Richard Rohr, OFM, is a Franciscan priest of the New Mexico Province and Founding Director of the Center for Action and Contemplation (CAC) in Albuquerque, New Mexico. An internationally recognized author and spiritual leader, Fr. Richard teaches primarily on incarnational mysticism, non-dual consciousness, and contemplation, with a particular emphasis on how these affect the social justice issues of our time.

Along with many recorded conferences, he is the author of numerous books, including *The Universal Christ* (2019), *Just This* (2018), *The Divine Dance* (2016), *Immortal Diamond* (2013), and *Falling Upward* (2012), all published by SPCK. To learn more about Fr. Richard Rohr and the CAC, visit https://cac.org/richard-rohr/richard-rohr-ofm/.

T0326767

RICHARD ROHR
the wisdom pattern

order
disorder
reorder

Originally published in the United States of America in 2001 as *Hope Against Darkness: The Transforming Vision of St. Francis in an Age of Anxiety* by Franciscan Media, 28 W. Liberty St., Cincinnati, OH 45202, www.FranciscanMedia.org

Revised US edition published in 2020 as *The Wisdom Pattern: Order, Disorder, Reorder*

Published in Great Britain in 2022

Society for Promoting Christian Knowledge
36 Causton Street
London SW1P 4ST
www.spck.org.uk

Scripture citations are taken from the *Jerusalem Bible*, copyright © 1966 by Darton, Longman & Todd Ltd., and Doubleday, a division of Random House, Inc., and from the *New Jerusalem Bible*, copyright © 1985 by Darton, Longman & Todd, Ltd., and Doubleday, a division of Random House, Inc. Reprinted by permission.

"The Great Chain of Being" was originally published in *Radical Grace* (the former newsletter for the Center for Action and Contemplation in Albuquerque, NM), October/November 1997, and the section entitled "What Is Behind Hate?" in Chapter Nine first appeared in *Radical Grace*, March/April 2000.

We are grateful to the following publishers for permission to reprint:
The Tablet, the international Catholic weekly, for excerpts from "Oh, to Be a Victim," by Andrew Greeley, copyright © 1997 by *The Tablet*.
Harcourt Brace Jovanovich and Faber and Faber for excerpts from "Burnt Norton" by T. S. Eliot, copyright © 1971 by Esme Valerie Eliot.
Paulist Press for excerpts from *Bonaventure*, Ewert Cousins, editor and translator, copyright © 1978.
Loretta Ross-Gotta for her poem "In Praise of Boundaries."

British Library Cataloguing-in-Publication Data
A catalogue record for this book is available from the British Library

ISBN 978-0-281-08661-0

1 3 5 7 9 10 8 6 4 2

Typeset by Falcon Oast Graphic Art Ltd
Printed and bound in Great Britain by Clays Ltd, Elcograf S.p.A.
Produced on paper from sustainable sources

Dedicated to Vanessa Guerin
for helping me to see what was always here.

Deus Meus et Omnia
My God—and *All* Things
—MOTTO OF THE FRANCISCANS

Contents

Acknowledgments

The author would like to acknowledge the inspiration and constant encouragement of Fr. Jeremy Harrington, OFM, and Sr. Pat Brockman, OSU.

This book began as part of the audiocassette series, *Rebuild the Church: Richard Rohr's Challenge for the New Millennium* (St. Anthony Messenger Press). Chapter Two was adapted from a talk Richard gave at the Archdiocese of Los Angeles Religious Education Congress in 1998. All of the material was rewritten, expanded, and somewhat reorganized for this second edition of the book. The author apologizes for any shortcomings from the transition from speech to the written word.

Preface to the Revised Edition

Instead of writing a discursive preface to re-introduce this book, I offer you a simple outline. Doing this made me realize I have been teaching much the same thing for most of my adult life:

Order, by itself, normally wants to eliminate any disorder and diversity, creating a narrow and cognitive rigidity in both people and systems.

Disorder, by itself, closes us off from any primal union, meaning, and eventually even sanity in both people and systems.

Reorder, or transformation of people and systems, happens when both are seen to work together.

The great spiritualities and philosophies often taught this quite directly, but with different vocabularies, symbols, and metaphors:

> Native peoples called it the cycle of Day > Night > Sunrise or Sun > Moon > Sun or Summer > Fall > Winter > Spring.

> Scientists speak of star > supernova explosion > vast amounts of light and energy.

> World mythologies present stories of Journey > Fall > Return to a new home.

> Religions often use some form of Birth > Sin > Rebirth or Law > Failure > Forgiveness or all is okay > Catastrophe > Hope.

The Wisdom Pattern

The Bible presents it as Garden of Eden > Fall > Paradise.

Walter Brueggemann teaches three kinds of Psalms: Psalms of Orientation > Psalms of Disorientation > Psalms of New Orientation.[1]

There are three sections to the Hebrew Scriptures: Law > Prophets > Wisdom.

Speakers and writers often refer to three steps forward and two steps backward.

Johann Fichte (1762–1814) called it thesis > antithesis > synthesis.[2]

George Ivanovich Gurdjieff (1866–1949) called it Holy Affirming > Holy Denying > Holy Reconciling.[3]

Philosophy speaks of Classic or Essentialism > Postmodern or Existentialism or Nihilism > Process or Evolutionary Philosophy.

Chemistry illustrates the pattern through solution > dissolution > resolution.

Paul Ricœur (1913–2005) spoke of First Naïveté > Complexity > Second Naïveté[4] or First Simplicity (dangerous) > Recalibration > Second Simplicity (enlightened).

The Recovery movement speaks of Innocence > Addiction > Recovery.

Many now just speak generally of construction > deconstruction > reconstruction.

Preface to the Revised Edition

Christians call it Life > Crucifixion > Resurrection.

Given the prevalence of this recurring theme, it must now be considered culpable blindness that most people still consider it somewhat of a surprise, a scandal, a mystery, or something to be avoided or overcome by an easy jump from stage one to stage three. This is human hubris and illusion. Progress is never a straight and uninterrupted line, but we have all been formed by the Western Philosophy of Progress that tells us it is, leaving us despairing and cynical.

This book, now largely re-edited through the loving work of Vanessa Guerin and Shirin McArthur, is our attempt to present this perennial philosophy in an updated version. We are indeed "saved" by knowing and surrendering to this universal pattern of reality. Knowing the full pattern allows us to let go of our first order, trust the disorder, and, sometimes even hardest of all—to trust the new reorder. Three big leaps of faith for all of us, and each of a different character.

PART ONE

The Current Dilemma

Before you speak of peace,
you must first have it
in your heart . . .

We have been called
to heal wounds,
to unite what
has fallen apart, and to bring home
any who have lost
their way.

—FRANCIS TO THE FIRST FRIARS,
Legend of the Three Companions, Number 58

PART ONE

The Current Dilemma

One

The Postmodern Opportunity

One reason so many people have lost heart today is that we feel both confused and powerless. The forces against us are overwhelming, including consumerism, racism, militarism, individualism, patriarchy, and the corporate juggernaut. These "powers and principalities" (Ephesians 6:12) seem to be fully in control. We feel helpless to choose our own lives, much less a common life, or to see any overarching meaning in it all.

This became all the more evident after the horrific terrorist attacks of September 11, 2001. Everything that had seemed so important—stock options, consumer choices, increasingly affluent lifestyles—suddenly faded. Church attendance increased immediately. Religious websites experienced a surge in activity. We saw a wave of patriotism unseen for decades. Some people even had the courage to look into our collective conscience and start questioning if the developed nations have been doing enough to help eradicate poverty worldwide.

In the two decades since 9/11, we have seen additional fractures develop in American society and around the world, along with global threats such as the COVID-19 pandemic. Patriotism has become divisive rather than inclusive. That surge in church attendance is a distant memory and smaller churches are further challenged as worship moves online through months of "social distancing." There is much less belief in the possibility of a common life than there was in the months after 9/11, although shelter-in-place is bringing out a few hopeful signs such as balcony singalongs and spontaneous online gatherings. It's clear that America is not the only country struggling with these issues. All of this points to a long-standing, deep need for social reconstruction that we must urgently address.

More than anything else, I believe, we are facing a crisis of meaning. The world seems so complex, and we seem so small. What can we do but let the waves of history carry us and try to keep afloat somehow?

Perhaps we can at least look to that same history for some patterns, or for those who found the patterns. That is the intention of this book. In that sense, this is a very traditional book, even though many of these patterns form revolutionary suggestions. I will point particularly to the man who has one of the longest bibliographies of anyone in history: an Italian friar called Francis of Assisi (1182–1226). He must have had some kind of genius to have attracted people in so many cultures and religions, and to seem contemporary in so many of his responses eight hundred years later.

Francis's Context and Reference Points

Saint Francis of Assisi stepped out into a world being recast by the emerging market economy. He lived amid a decaying old order in which his father was greedily buying up the small farms of debtors and moving quickly into the new entrepreneurial class. Francis stepped into a church that seems to have been largely out of touch with the masses. He trusted a deeper voice and a bigger truth. He sought one clear center and moved out from there.

His one clear centerpiece was the Incarnate Jesus. Francis understood everything else from that personalized reference point. Like Archimedes, Francis had found his one firm spot on which to stand and from which he could move his world. He did this in at least three clear ways.

First, he walked into the prayer-depths of his own tradition, as opposed to mere religious repetition of old formulas. Second, he sought direction in the mirror of creation itself, as opposed to mental and fabricated ideas or ideals. Third, and most radically, he looked to the underside of his society, to the *community of those who had suffered*, for an understanding of how God transforms us. In other words, he found *depth and breadth—and a process to keep us there.*

The depth was an inner life where all shadow, mystery, and paradox were confronted, accepted, and forgiven. Here, he believed God could be met in fullness and truth. The breadth was the actual world itself, a sacramental universe. It was not the ideal, the churchy, or the mental, but the right-in-front-of-us-and-everywhere—the *actual* as opposed to the ideal.

Francis also showed us the process for staying there—the daring entrance into the world of human powerlessness. His chosen lens was what he called "poverty" and, of course, he was only imitating Jesus. He set out to read reality through the eyes and authority of those who have suffered and been rejected—and come out resurrected. This is apparently the *privileged seeing* that allows us to know something that we can know in no other way. It is the unique baptism with which Jesus says we must all be baptized (see Mark 10:39). My assumption in this book is that this is the baptism that transforms. It is larger than any religion or denomination. It is taught by the Spirit in and through reality itself.

We can argue doctrinally about many aspects of Jesus's life and teaching, but we cannot say he was not a poor man, or that he did not favor the perspective from the bottom as a privileged viewpoint. All other heady arguments about Jesus must deal with this overwhelming fact. Francis did. This perspective became his litmus test for all orthodoxy and for ongoing transformation into God.

For Francis, the true "I" had, first of all, to be discovered and realigned (the prayer journey into the True Self). Then he had to experience himself situated inside of a meaning-filled cosmos (a sacramental universe). Finally, he had to be poor (to be able to read reality from the side of powerlessness).

Francis taught us, therefore, that the antidote to confusion and paralysis is always a return to simplicity, to what is actually right in front of us, to the nakedly obvious. Somehow, he had the genius to reveal what was hidden in plain sight. It was so simple that it was hard to get there, and it will take the rest of this book to explain such simplicity!

The Age of the Mind

How did we get so far from Francis's world? What we call the modern age emerged in the eighteenth-century Enlightenment. It was the age of rationalism. The Enlightenment produced a wonderfully scientific mind. Its materialist worldview taught us how to measure things. Belief hinged on what could be proven by a certain paradigm called science. Science assumed—and this became the arrogance of the modern mind—that it knew more than anybody else ever had. It did not yet realize that this new knowing was limited to small areas. In its newfound excitement, such knowing quickly neglected other areas. Analysis of parts became more important than a synthesis of the whole.

We have been dazzled by our new abilities to know for three centuries now. The modern mind is enthralled with its ability to make things happen, to rearrange genes, chromosomes, and atoms. Being able to predict outcomes feels like an almost godly power—and it is. It led us to a philosophy of progress, as opposed to most cyclic or paschal worldviews.

Asia is the source of most great religions. In that more harmonious worldview, death and life (along with everything else) need to be kept in balance. In contrast, we prefer to think that we can overcome the death mystery. Modern people believe that things will only get better and better. This worldview has taken many surrogate forms and shaped all of us deeply, especially in the West. It told us that education, reason, and science would make the world a better place.

But then the Holocaust happened—in the very country that was perhaps the most educated, logical, and reason-loving in the world. For Europeans, the collapse into postmodern thinking began at that point: "If we can be this wrong, maybe nothing is right. All our major institutions failed us."

For Americans, by reason of our isolation from the absurdity of war, our immense power, and our incorrigible innocence, we remained in the modern era until the late 1960s. I remember teachers in primary school telling me in the 1950s that we would have overcome all major diseases by the turn of the twenty-first century. It has not turned out that way, as we all know. Now, in fact, we have a lot of new physical diseases and many unsolvable diseases of the mind and soul.

For the last fifty years, we've begun to speak not of *modernism* but of *postmodernism*—a critique of modernism's false optimism and trust in progress. We're in the postmodern period now, at least in Europe and North America and those countries influenced by them (which is, for better or worse, almost every country). We now see that reading reality simply through the paradigm of science, reason, and technological advancement has not served us well. It has not served the soul well. It has not served the heart or the psyche well. It has not served community well. There must be something more than the physical, because mere science has left us powerful and effective, but also ravaged in the most important areas of our humanity. The inner world of meaning has not been fed.

The soul, the psyche, and human relationships seem at this point to be destabilizing at an almost exponential rate. Our society is producing very many unhappy and unhealthy people. The spread of violence throughout society is frightening. We're seeing that the postmodern mind forms a deconstructed world-view. It does not know what it is *for*, as much as it knows what it is *against* and what it *fears*. To have a positive vision of life is almost considered naïve in most intellectual circles. Such folks are not taken seriously. They are considered fools.

If we cannot trust in what we thought was logic and reason, if science is not able to create a totally predictable universe, then *maybe there are no patterns*. Suddenly we live in a very scary and even dis-enchanted universe—where no intelligence appears to be in charge, where there is no beginning, middle, or end.

What's left is merely the private ego with its own attempts at episodic meaning and control. We find this in the postmodern novel, deconstructivist art, and movies with aimless direction and gratuitous violence. This is the world in which most of those living today were formed. It is starved for meaning, grasping at anything and everything.

To Know and Not to Know

The postmodern mind assumes that nothing is truly knowable, that everything is a social or intellectual construct that will soon be discounted by new information. The irony is that the same postmodernist also believes that he or she knows more than anybody else—that there are no absolutes, no patterns that are always true. We end up with a being who is both god-like ("I know") and utterly cynical ("I have to create my own truth because there are no universal patterns"). This is a terrible dilemma with which to live. It is an impossible burden which earlier generations never presumed to carry. No wonder depression and suicide now affect even children's lives to such a degree!

Postmodern thinking allows us to discredit and discount everything, which also leaves us in a lonely and absurd state. Philosophically, it's called nihilism—*nihil* meaning "nothing." Nihilism affects us all in some way, but most especially those at the top and the bottom of any society. The elite have the freedom to dismiss and discount everything beneath them. The oppressed finally have an explanation for their sad state. We see this tragedy in most of the minority and oppressed groups of the world, and in the addictive entertainment culture of the wealthy. For the rich it's a false high, for the poor a false low, and both are losing.

Stephen Carter, a first-rate cultural critic, accuses many of his own black brothers and sisters and all of America of holding a nihilistic and inevitably materialistic worldview, except for those who have held onto their religious roots.[5] We could say this of most Western groups, but only a black brother could say it of his own. He says there's no belief in anything except power, possessions, and prestige in America, despite a religious façade. Michael Lerner, a Jewish philosopher and psychologist, says much the same to his audience.[6]

Another aspect of the postmodern mind is what we call a "market" mentality. In a market-driven culture like ours, things no longer have *inherent value*, but only *exchange value*. "Will it sell? Will it win? Will it defeat the opponent?" These are the first concerns, and sometimes the only concerns, of the *market mind*. It leaves us very empty and shapeless after a few years, while still motivating us for another day. The "temple" of creation has then become a place of mere buying and selling. No wonder Jesus was driven to rage at such a scene, and consciously made "a whip out of cord" to drive it out (see John 2:15).

Once we lose a sense of inherent value, we have lost all hope of encountering true value, much less the Holy. Even religious people, if they do not pray, will normally regress to an exchange-value reading of religion. It is no longer about the Great Mystery, mystic union, and transformation, but merely social order and control. Moral codes and priesthoods are enlisted for the sake of enforcement and some measure of civility. For many, if not most, Western Christians, it is basically a crime-and-punishment scenario, instead of the grace-and-mercy world that Jesus proclaims.

This is the only way that the postmodern Christian can hope to give shape to this basically shapeless story called human life. It looks like an answer, or even gospel, but it is the same old story line of most of history: The big and strong win; Prometheus passes for Jesus. I must admit this was the only gospel I heard in my early seminary training. What a relief to finally study the Gospels and observe the real transformative patterns in humanity!

The final state of a nihilistic worldview is a collapse into vulgarity and shock as the primary values. If there is no criterion of quality, we can at least compensate with quantity (of emotion, violence, sex, sound), which normally devolves into a deep dismissal of almost everything. Soon the concern becomes: "How can I be more outrageous than anyone else?" "How can I laugh at things before they disappoint me?" There are no heroes or heroines, so the individual feels a kind of negative heroism in exposing all human failings, foibles, and phoniness. I do not really have to grow up myself; I will find my meaning in pointing out that everyone and everything else is phony.

Let's admit that this is the character of much of our political life too. We are all pulling one another downward in such a scenario, but it is not the downward mobility of humility. It is merely the downward spiral of a universal skepticism.

Strangely, this is almost a secular form of Puritanism. We are still trying to expose and hate the sins of the world; they are just defined differently. The sex scandals of Washington are not much different from the old Irish priests preoccupied with ferreting out fornicators in the parish. We think we can dominate the shadow self rather than forgive it, transform it, and embrace it into a larger wholeness. No wonder Jesus did not concentrate on the shadow self at all, but almost entirely on the ego!

It is much easier to look for someone to blame, sue, expel, or expose when there is no coherent meaning or divine purpose in the world. Someone has to be at fault for my unhappy life! As long as we keep trying to deal with the mystery of evil in some way other than forgiveness and healing, we will continue to create negative ideologies like fundamentalism and nihilism in all their endless forms. One demands perfect order; the other denies that it is even possible. Jesus does neither, but lives on the horns of the human dilemma.

We've all seen things in recent years that not long ago we would have considered unthinkable. These spectacles are not limited to gangster rappers or cultural dropouts by any means. This trend has shown itself in mainstream art and media, in writing, in our political life, and in every aspect of lifestyle. We are no longer expected to submit to the classic disciplines of anything, because there aren't any.

It is one thing to endure the years of discipline that it takes to learn a craft, and then to put paint on paper in new and creative ways. That might, in some cases, rise to great art. *We have to know the rules before we can break the rules.* "Breaking the rules," after all, is often the source of genuine creativity and even genuine holiness. But starting there— throwing paint on the paper as a form of self-expression—is not going to stand the test of time. There's nothing there that is tied into collective memory or the archetypal anything. It is just "*my* feelings." There is too much of the imperial ego and too little room for anybody else, for anything communal and shareable.

Private feelings are our form of truth today, a kind of ultimate self-absorption—understandable because there are *no universal patterns*. Yet, in expressing private feelings, people really think they've done something great. We see this on the talk shows. We realize those people have never read, studied, prayed, or listened to anybody except their own tyrannical feelings. Yet they think they have a right for their *un*informed opinions on the welfare system or religion or nuclear warfare to be taken seriously! No wonder our public discourse is deteriorating, even at the level of the court, the senate, the university, and, yes, the church.

It is true that lots of folks are angry and alienated and have something to say about it, but we've got to listen to some greater minds, some greater hearts, some greater souls who are not just caught in their own self-expression ("this is me") but are also addressing the greater issues ("this is us") and, especially, the Great Patterns that are always true. (I will discuss these terms more fully in Chapter Five.) Those are the people who will reconstruct. Those are the people worth listening to and talking with. I think that is what it means to be a part of the great human parade instead of just an isolated individual, a member of the Cosmic Body of Christ instead of being designated by that oxymoron: "an individual believer."

If you are an individualist you are surely not a believer, and if you are a believer you are utterly responsible, connected, and aligned everywhere. Before we can reconstruct this deconstructed culture, we must be utterly reconnected our-selves. That is the work of healthy religion (*re-ligio* = "re-bind"). Maybe that is another way to describe our inherent need to submit to classic patterns.

Owning Our Cultural Biases

Every viewpoint is a view from a point. Unless we recognize and admit our own personal and cultural viewpoints, we will never know how to decentralize our own perspective, and we will live with a high degree of illusion and blindness that brings much suffering into the world. I think this is what Simone Weil (1909–1943) meant in saying that the love of God is the source of all truth. Only an outer and positive reference point utterly grounds the mind—or the heart, for that matter.

One of the keys to wisdom is that we must recognize our own biases, our own addictive preoccupations, and those things to which, for some reason, we refuse to pay attention. Until we see these patterns (which is early stage contemplation), we will never be able to *see what we do not see*. No wonder that Saint Teresa of Ávila (1515–1582) declared self-knowledge to be the first and necessary entrance way to the Interior Castle.[7] Without such critical awareness of the small self, there is little chance that any individual will produce truly great knowing or endur-ing wisdom.

Postmodernism, in a rage of disappointment, is deconstructing everything in its path to counter the three controlling presuppos-itions of modernism which formed our age. (As we will see, deconstruction is having both good and bad effects. We must say up front that there are good meanings to deconstruction!

Without some deconstruction, everything becomes idolatrous. The prophets were religious deconstructionists.)

First, modernism believed that *reality is ordered*. Postmodern thought says there is no order at all. Postmodernism, ironically, is moving closer to both nihilism and mysticism, to the notion that either *no one* is in charge or *someone else* is in charge. All we know is that our logic and reason clearly is not! Hence the new rise in spiritualities of every style and stripe. Churches have lots of competition, whereas they used to have a monopoly.

It strikes me as not accidental that we called priesthood "Holy Orders." The term seems to reveal what we really wanted from priesthood: order, lines of order, boundaries, control, clarity. These are not bad qualities of themselves, even much-needed qualities, but the desire for them might explain why even the church was more comfortable with the assumptions of modernism than with this "holy disorder" now showing itself. Yet, the cross itself is clearly a proclamation of *disorder* at the heart of reality. True Christianity never believed in either perfect order or total chaos, but a reality fraught with contradictions. It made this mixed world the world of God. Jesus was crucified on the collision of opposites.

Second, the modern mind believed that *reality is knowable by our human reason*. Nature is predictable and, therefore, to some degree controllable. Quantum physics, however, now says that indeterminacy, probability, chaos theories, and Heisenberg's uncertainty principle perhaps more truly express the final mystery of reality than classical physics ever did.

This is a great humiliation for the modern mind. Physics has discovered that when we get to the smallest points (atomic

particles) and the biggest points (galaxies and black holes)—
it's mystery again! It looks knowable, yet finally it's unknowable
when we reach the edges. Control eventually gives way to
mystery and the letting go of control. Suddenly, we are not in
charge. Some say that the physicists are becoming mystics,
while the clergy are becoming psychologists—both trying to
figure out the non-rational responses of most people and the
tragic character of most events.

The small scientist stays in the middle and thinks he or she
is living inside an entirely coherent system. The great scientists
like Einstein, the "Man of the (20th) Century," enter back into
mystery. Einstein said, "The most beautiful and profound experience is the feeling of mystery."[8] He never had the arrogance
to think he had fully discovered his Unified Field Theory, the
final paradigm that would account for all the forces in the universe. His humble assertion is the act of faith of a great mind, a
great scientist. It reminds me of the image Dante (c. 1265–1321)
used for the heights of paradise: a white rose. Utter simplicity
and utter beauty. It coheres. It holds together. That sense of
coherence is what we no longer have.

Great religion always said that the best we could hope for
would be metaphor, symbol, and image. Here, we do not know as
much as *we are known*; we do not make the connections as much
as realize that *we are connected*. Then we can only kneel and kiss
the ground. The logical mind gives up its tyranny.

Deconstructivism, as terrible as it sounds, might well be
leading us to the proper humility and simplicity for truly healthy
God-encounters. Yet, the churches, at least the Roman Church,
had grown used to a philosopher's God much more than the

biblical God, who scandalizes us with particularity, preferences, choices, and absolute freedom. Modernism gave us predictability that felt good; now someone else is in charge and we must surrender to both tragedy and utter gratuity. It sounds much more biblical, even if also much more frightening.

Third, the modern mind believed that *human fulfillment consisted primarily in knowing and discovering all the laws of science and nature*. Modernism said we should utilize them whenever possible and comply with them when we can't know them or change them. In order to move ahead, therefore, all we had to do was increase scientific knowledge. Whether it be medical knowledge or space exploration, we would overcome all difficulty.

Anyone born before 1960 was deeply influenced by that kind of thinking, but we no longer believe it, nor that mere education transforms people. We no longer are so sure that the laws of nature are predictable and that human nature consists in knowing all the laws and controlling the universe as best we can. If you doubt this, simply look at the emergence of superstition and magic, UFO theories, New Age fundamentalism of every sort, shamanic journeys, and an actual reveling in the unconscious, the irrational, the non-rational, the symbolic, and the "spiritual"—and much of this among very educated people! The gods of the body, belly, and heart are demanding to be heard, not just the god of reason.

There's bad news and good news here. Living in a transitional age is scary: It's falling apart, it's unknowable, it doesn't cohere, it doesn't make sense, it's all mystery again, and we can't put order in it. This is the postmodern panic. It lies beneath most of our cynicism, our anxiety, and our pandemic violence.

Yet, there is little in the biblical revelation that ever promised us an ordered universe. The whole Bible is about meeting God in the *actual*, in the incarnate moment, in the scandal of particularity, and not in educated theories—so much so that it is rather amazing that we ever tried to codify and control the whole thing.

The Bible seems to always be saying that this life is indeed a journey, a journey always initiated and concluded by God, and a journey of transformation much more than mere education about anything. We would sooner have textbooks, I think. Then the journey would remain a spectator sport, as much of religion often seems to be. The education model elicits a low level of commitment and investment, even if it keeps people obedient and orthodox. The transformation model risks people knowing and sharing "the One Spirit that was given us all to drink" (1 Corinthians 12:13). So sad that we have preferred conformity and group loyalty over real change!

But chaos often precedes great creativity. Darkness creates the desire for light. Faith actually precedes great leaps into new knowledge. That's the good news. Our uncertainty is the doorway into mystery, the doorway into surrender, the path to God that Jesus called "faith." (How strange, and actually heresy of the first order, that we turned this dark night of faith into a demand for certitude and control!) I'm seeing people of great faith today, people of the Big Truth, who love the church but are no longer on bended knee before an idol. They don't need to worship the institution; neither do they need to throw it out and react against it. This is a great advance in human maturity. We are slowly discovering what many of us are calling the

Third Way, neither fight nor flight, but the way of compassionate knowing.

Both the way of fight and the way of flight fall short of wisdom, although they look like answers in the heat of the moment. When it's an either/or world, we have no ability to transcend, to hold together, to be creative.

The dualistic mind seemingly has a preference for knowing things by comparison. The price we pay for our dualistic mind is that one side of the comparison is always idealized and the other demonized, or at least minimized. There is little room for balance or honesty, much less love. Wisdom, however, is always holding the "rational" and the "romantic" together: Aristotle and Plato, Aquinas and Bonaventure, Freud and Jung, saint and sinner, Spirit and senses.

In fact, we could say that the greater the opposites we can hold together, the greater soul we usually have. By temperament, most of us prefer one side to the other. Holding to one side or another frees us from the tension and the anxiety. Only a few dare to hold the irresolvable tension in the middle. It is the "folly" of the cross, where we cannot *prove* we are right, but only *hang* between the good and the bad thieves of every issue, paying the price for their reconciliation (see Luke 23:39–43).

The *tertium quid*, the "reconciling third," is very often the Holy Spirit—but, as many have said before, the Holy Spirit is the rejected or forgotten member of the Holy Trinity. We don't know how to dogmatize or control wind, water, or doves alighting from the sky (see John 3:8). Such deliberate and daring metaphors for God should keep us rightly humble in all our knowing, predicting, and explaining.

The Mysterium Tremendum

For Christians, the abandonment of modernism's certainty is going to be a journey deeper into both biblical religion and the *tremendous mystery* of Jesus. He is the archetype of what it means to be a full human being. He holds together heaven and earth, divine and human, a male body with a female soul. He is a living example of full consciousness, which is precisely to accept the usually rejected unconscious, fear-filled, and shadowy parts of reality. He's the son of God and the son of Adam. We need to realize that we also are daughters of God and daughters of earth, of divinity and of flesh, of ego and of shadow. Both are good, and they are even better when they are put together. That's why we follow Jesus! He is the icon of what salvation means. When the two can happily coexist within us, one might say that we are "saved."

Our goal ought to be a spirituality connected to this world in every aspect, seeing the Divine Light shining through the mundane, the ordinary, the physical, the material, the entire cosmos—and not only in the churchy, the correct, and the pure, which keeps the world split and contentious. That's the synthesis toward which I believe healthy Christianity is leading us. "When that day comes, the very bells on the horses will be inscribed with the words, 'Sacred to Yahweh,' and the cooking pots of the house of Yahweh will be as holy as the sprinkling bowls before the altar" (Zechariah 14:20).

The Apostle Paul intuits this when he speaks in Ephesians (4:4–6) of "one Body, one Spirit . . . one hope . . . one Lord, one faith, one baptism, and one God who is Father of all, over all, through all, and within all." Yet, if I talked that way today, I would be accused in many Catholic circles of pantheism or lightweight humanism—so I just quote Paul.

We have no reason to apologize for our Christ. He is a flawless image, especially in his crucified and risen form, of all that God is doing on earth. He is our living icon of transformation. Jesus holds together the tension of opposites, in their ultimate shapes of life and death. *Humanity itself could be defined as that which is eternally crucified and eternally resurrected—all at once!*

The cross, as we will see again and again, is the "coincidence of opposites": One movement going vertical, another going horizontal, clearly at cross-purposes. When the opposing energies of any type collide within us, we suffer. If we agree to hold them creatively until they transform us, it becomes redemptive suffering. This stands in clear and total opposition to the myth of redemptive violence, which has controlled most of human history, even though it has never redeemed anything. Expelling the contradictions instead of *forgiving* them only perpetuates the problem. This is so obvious and self-evident that most people cannot see it. Maybe that is why John's Gospel seems to make blindness the primary metaphor for sin.

We're living in a time when the far right and the far left in almost every institution are using the eccentricities and evils of the other end to justify their own extremes. There seems to be an emergence of reactionary and protectionist thinking all over the world, which then serves as justification for people's overreacting on the political left. This ping-pong game has been so common in both the twentieth and twenty-first centuries, even within Christianity—which should know better by now—that

Christianity, for many, has come to mean anti-intellectual, fanatically narrow-minded people. Christianity, for some, is neither faith nor reason—just reactive tribalism hiding behind the skirts of Mother Church. How sad it would be if the Great Tradition ever settled for so little.

I move in some circles where the word *Christian*, unfortunately, is a negative adjective. To them, "He's a Christian" means he knows nothing about history, nothing about politics, and is probably incapable of civil conversation about anything. Five Bible quotes are the available answers to everything. How did we ever get to this low point after developing such a tradition of wisdom? How did we ever regress to such arrogance after the humble folly of the cross?

When there is no ability to build bridges to the other, or to even understand otherness, we know we are outside the pale of authentic Christianity. Surely Jesus came for more than self-congratulative societies who forever circle the wagons around their own saved identity and their own self-serving god!

Such trivializations of God's greatness deserve to be ignored and avoided, even when the churches themselves get involved in such partisanship. Don't waste time fighting it directly or you will become its casualty. Our motto is simple and clear: *The best criticism of the bad is the practice of the better.* Just go ahead and live positively, "in God, through God, with God." In time, the fruits will be apparent. In the short run, you will hold the unresolved tension of the cross. In the long run, you will usher in something entirely new and healing. This was the almost intuitive spiritual genius of Saint Francis. He wasted no time attacking the rich churches and pretentious clergymen, or even greedy tradesmen like his dad; he just went to the side and did life differently. He is remembered forever; they are lost to history.

A Lonesome World

I'll conclude this chapter with a look at a sad by-product of post-modernism: loneliness. Postmodernism and modernism reject a personalized universe. They *dis-enchant* the universe. We no longer expect miracles. We no longer expect the transcendent to shine through the tree and the leaf, with "every common bush afire with God."[9] This is our modern state of alienation and anxiety, what the French call *ressentiment*. One aspect of *ressentiment* describes a world that is no longer safe, no longer sacred, and no longer home. It is disconnected, fragile, and, therefore, always ready to take offense. The experience of the alienated member of society is "I'm alone" and "I have to figure it all out." The secular world is no longer abundant enough or safe enough to imagine a win/win scenario. Everything is zero sum—all winding down. Our world's only story line is win/lose, but unfortunately it actually ends up being lose/lose.

Yet, this very secular and empty worldview longs for the opposite. Have you noticed how often the media has covered religious stories, angels, saints, and miracles during the past few years? American Greetings, one of the largest greeting-card companies, added a line of spiritual and religious cards, noting a "new trend" in America. We know this world is too dead, too empty, too disenchanted—it's not enough for us. We're not at home without our spiritual nature.

Some understanding of this often comes together for people very clearly at the end of their lives. I was with my mother when she passed away. At one point before her death, she was seeing angels. Now, my mother was no sentimentalist. She was an Enneagram Eight, a Kansan earth woman, and an utter realist. I probably got my no-nonsense Catholicism from her. But, about a week before she died, she started seeing angels, even my guardian angel. (When we get close to the end, they say the veil gets very thin between the worlds.)

My mother, at the end, would use the word *home* so much. She'd tell my father to come over to her sickbed and then say, "Take me home." He thought she wanted him to drive her across town to her house, since she spent her final days at my brother's house. After a while, we understood that home meant something different.

The sadness of modern people is that we don't feel at home. No wonder we have Doctor Kevorkians. Euthanasia, abortion, capital punishment, and war itself will only increase unless there's a larger story like the paschal mystery that gives transcendent meaning to human suffering. The soul must expand, it seems, so that we can carry the great mystery of God. We must "learn to bear the beams of love," as William Blake would say.[10] That learning is usually, I am sorry to say, in the realm of suffering. It seems to be the only thing strong enough to make us surrender control and what we call logic.

God makes grace out of our grit, salvation out of our sin. We are saved, ironically, not by doing it right as much as by the suffering of having done it wrong. We come to God not through our perfection (thank God!) as much as through our imperfection. Finally, all must be forgiven and reconciled. Life does not have to be fixed, controlled, or even understood for us to be happy. That is good news! In fact, what else would it be?

The gospel is a new "logic" that "The Fool on the Hill," as in the Lennon and McCartney song, brought to the world. This gospel logic is much broader, much deeper, much more spacious and filled with compassion than any system of thought that the world has been able to create. Maybe that is what truth means. Why would anyone settle for the small mind of rationalism or the no-mind of non-rationalism? This is the Great Mind of Christ.

Two

Beyond Victimhood

Many people in many parts of our world are clearly carrying the cross today. For those in poverty, perhaps it is the cross of deep social injustice. For us in affluent countries, it's more likely that we carry the crosses of broken relationships and broken psyches. What I find we hold in common is that, for most people, it doesn't feel like the cross. It just feels like pain.

Every age has had its pain, and spirituality, in its best sense, is about *what we do with our pain*. We do not know what to do with it anymore. The "machine" that transformed our pain into something better seems to have disappeared. In a culture with no Transcendent Center, there is no one to whom we can hand over the pain. In a culture with no cross-and-resurrection image, there is no meaning to our suffering. When a people no longer knows that God *is*, God is *good*, God can be *trusted*, and God is *on our side*, we frankly have very serious problems. Our pain will go shooting out in all directions, none of them good. That's where we are today.

A woman once came to me for spiritual direction who, by her own admission, was becoming a rather hateful and negative person, both in her family and in her job. In the time that we met, she kept coming back to this seemingly irresolvable pain, this injustice that she had experienced, rightly or wrongly, truthfully or untruthfully. In one moment, an admission slipped out of her mouth: "My pain is my ticket." As we talked it through, I realized, and I think she did too, that her pain had become her very identity. She seemed to know that playing the victim gave her a kind of power, an instant moral superiority over almost everybody. Strangely, she had become untouchable and invulnerable.

Although individuals have probably often done this, it is only in the last fifty years that it has become a cultural fad. Now we even have inherited victimhood. People gain all kinds of immediate credit because somebody's great-grandmother did something to their great-grandmother's generation.

This is probably the ultimate form of moral blackmail. All we have to do, in this strange configuration of life, is prove that we are a victim and we immediately have the moral high ground. We can also cop out and do nothing, because we now carry this paralyzing wound. In either case, we stop growing and make life miserable for everyone around us.

Playing the victim is an effective way of getting moral high ground without doing any moral development whatsoever. We don't have to grow up, we don't have to let go, we don't have to forgive, we don't have to surrender—all the things that great religion has deemed necessary. Now we just have to accuse somebody else of being worse than we are, or of being a member of a race or group that is worse than ours, and that makes us feel like we're good, moral, or superior. To prove that someone else is a sinner gives us the strange belief—obviously not true—that we are above all that sort of thing.

Let me give several examples from "Oh, to Be a Victim," an essay by Andrew Greeley.[11] (Don't be offended too quickly: If you could read all the way through, you would see that the article doesn't try to take one side or the other of any contemporary issue. Rather, it shows how we can all play the victim on either side of any issue to seek moral high ground.)

Victimhood, for Greeley, is a twist on the old sin of pride.

> "I am from the Third World. You are from the First World. You have exploited us for centuries. Therefore you are guilty of exploitation, indeed of exploiting me. Therefore I am morally superior to you and have power in our relationship."[12]

This is a form of power, but it's not the power that Jesus is offering us from the cross. Here is another:

> "I am a woman. You are a man. Men have oppressed women always. Therefore you [as an individual man] are an oppressor. In fact you are oppressing me. Confess your guilt, not that it will do you any good."[13]

That's a little unfair, but he wants to give us the feeling, I guess.

> "I am an African American. You are a white American. Your ancestors brought mine here as slaves. You are responsible for the sufferings of African Americans and for my suffering. Do not try to defend yourself. As a white person you are by definition a racist." . . .

> "I am Jewish. You are German. Your ancestors killed my people. You must acknowledge your guilt for what they

did and your moral inferiority to me. You claim that your ancestors died in a German concentration camp? That will do you no good. The German nation was and is responsible for the Holocaust. You are presumed to be anti-Semitic and don't try to prove yourself innocent because you can't."

"I am a Native American. You are a white American. Your people committed genocide against my people. You must confess your own personal responsibility for that sin and concede me my moral superiority." . . .

"I am gay. You are straight. Therefore I am morally superior to you."

"I am a Palestinian Arab. You are Jewish. Therefore I am morally superior to you."[14]

And on and on and on. Victims have found a way to be superior. The rest of us must concede them moral power—at least if they are fashionable victims. Fashion, as we all know, changes every few years.

Although it has become a uniquely American form of entitlement, victimhood does not work in much of the rest of the world. I suspect it would only emerge where the gospel has at least been heard (introducing empathy for the victim) and can now be turned around to personal advantage. It probably only works where people are also rather rich and individualistic, jockeying for power in superficial ways. But it's clearly a major distortion of the cross that hangs in churches and homes across the land.

The cross became the Center for Action and Contemplation's company logo. It is more than something *upon which we gazed* and *by which we were transformed. Jesus neither played the victim nor created victims. He became a saving and forgiving victim.*

Inherited and entitled victimhood will get us nowhere. It simply keeps us playing the old game of power in a new, very subtle and disturbing way. It is not the way of powerlessness that Jesus taught us from the cross. It is pretending to be powerless, but, in fact, for the sake of power and control over others. It is the disguise and deterioration of the beautiful, and always scary, message of Jesus. Half of the message is often more problematic than total ignorance. Half of the message safely inoculates us from the whole, while total ignorance leaves us wide open for conversion. Thus, we have Jesus's shocking statements about the Reign of God welcoming prostitutes and sinners (Matthew 21:31), who knew they were "out of it." We call this "beginner's mind," and it is always a head-start, spiritually speaking.

The pattern in most of history, and even unfortunately today, has been somewhat different. Most human pain has been transmitted to others. It is normally easier to expel our anxiety and our shame by projecting it onto somebody else. "Let them carry it. I don't want to," we say unconsciously—and it sort of works! We feel relieved by having an enemy or a problem out there. It gives us focus and identity.

René Girard (1923–2015) wrote that this scapegoating mechanism can be seen as the central story line of human history, a subject to which we will return. In fact, the list of wars and "who killed who" is what most people have called history! We never cared much about herstory, or the story of those who physically built the pyramids, or the stories from the side of the losers. (That, by the way, is what is so unique about much of the Bible.)

One of the few generalizations we can make in the field of universal spirituality is this: *No one else is your problem.* You are always the locus of conversion and transformation. It is always about *you* first of all—always. You can even use that as a good litmus test for authentic spirituality. Is it keeping you listening for God? Is it keeping your own feet to the fire? Then it is probably healthy teaching. Is it leading you to suspicion, paranoia, accusation, and blaming? Then it is from the "Accuser," which is a quite significant New Testament name for Satan (Revelation 12:10). The Evil One is not only an Accuser, therefore, but also a "father of lies" (John 8:44), because the other one is not your problem, even though Evil would prefer to have you think so. It keeps you from your own needed transformation and keeps the contentious spirit alive.

Jesus did the victim thing right. He neither played the victim for his own self-aggrandizement nor did he make victims of other people. He became the liberating and forgiving victim. This pattern is quite rare, but, whenever it happens, it exercises an immense healing and reconciling influence, even though it often increases the wrath and denial of some accusers. Just read the lives of Martin Luther King, Jr., Oscar Romero, or Mahatma Gandhi for the most visible examples from our recent past. Normally, the prophets are killed because they bring the lie out into the open. At that point, our hatred is pointed toward the messenger, because he or she has taken away our needed object of hatred. If we need to hate, we will destroy anyone who tells us our hatred is the problem.

The message of the crucified Jesus is a statement about *what to do with our pain now*. What we've done, for some strange reason, is make Jesus into the one who could keep us from pain *later*. We've missed the entire transformative message! Now it is only a message of gambling and bargaining with God, and attending religious services, often for people with low-level resentment who clearly do not want to be there (ask any parish priest!). Somehow, Jesus becomes the great problem-solver and answer-giver for the next world and not primarily the one who teaches us how to live with peace and freedom in this world. It's fire-insurance religion instead of a banquet right now. That is a big, big difference— an entirely different agenda.

In the final book of the Bible, the Book of Revelation, we have this recurring image of the Lamb of God (for example, 5:6). He stands on the altar in the center of a cosmic liturgy. Christians are familiar with this symbol: the lamb who is *simultaneously* slaughtered and standing. That paradox is the message of the gospel, the message of the cross: We are simultaneously—in one and the same moment—slaughtered and victorious. Once we could hardly find an older church which did not have this image somewhere in the liturgical space, and yet I wonder how many people ever understood its archetypal meaning, and why it was the key to opening the seven seals usually draped underneath. The lamb image reveals *the lie of ignorant killing* that has characterized most of human history—and, even more, it gives us a way out.

Zealots and Pharisees

As noted earlier, there seem to be two common avoidances of conversion or transformation, two typical diversionary tactics that we humans use to avoid holding the pain: fight or flight.

The way of *fight* is what I'll call the way of Simon the zealot, and often the way of the cultural liberal. These folks want to change, fix, control, and reform other people and events. The zealot is always looking for the evil, the political sinner, the unjust one, the oppressor, or the bad person *over there*. The zealot permits himself or herself to righteously attack them, to hate them, even to kill them. When they do, they think they are "doing a holy duty for God" (John 16:2).

It is a general rule that *when we don't transform our pain we will always transmit it*. Zealots and contemporary liberals often have the right conclusion, but their tactics and motives are frequently filled with self, power, control, and the same righteousness that they hate in conservatives. Basically, they want to *do something* to avoid holding the pain until it transforms them. Because of this too-common pattern, I have come to mistrust almost all righteous indignation and moral outrage. In my experience, it is hardly ever from God.

"Resurrected" people prayerfully bear witness against injustice and evil—but also agree compassionately to hold their own complicity in that same evil. It is not over there, it is here. It is *our* problem, not *theirs*. The Risen Christ, not accidentally, still carries the wounds of the crucifixion in his hands and side.

We've all been there at different times. I know I've been there: Trying to drive out "the devil" with my own "prince of devils" (see Luke 11:14–22). We're actually energized by having an enemy, someone to hate, because it takes away the inner shame and relieves our inner anxiety.

It gives us, strangely enough, a very false sense of control and superiority, because we've spotted the evil and, thank God, it's over there. As long as *they* are the problem and we can keep our focus on changing them, correcting them, expelling them as the contaminating element, then we can sit in a reasonably comfortable position. But it's a position that the saints called *pax perniciosa*, a dangerous and false peace. It feels like peace, but it's not a true peace. It is the peace of avoidance, denial, and projection. The peace of the Crucified comes from holding the tension; the dangerous peace comes from expelling it elsewhere or denying the pain. Yet, to the untrained, the latter feels like peace.

It has taken us a long time to realize that we cannot afford to hate because we become a mirror or disguised image of the same. Once we let the other determine the energy and agenda, we can only react to it, and soon we are using the same energy and the same agenda, but we can't see it.

This leads us to the second diversionary tactic: the way of *flight*. This is the common path of the Pharisee, the uninformed, the falsely innocent, and often the conservative type. They deny the pain altogether. They refuse to carry the shadow side of anything, in themselves or in their chosen groups. There will be no uncertainty, no ambiguity. There will be no problems. It is a form of narcotic, and sometimes probably necessary to get through the day.

But the flight people are also subject to hypocrisy, projection, or just plain illusion: "We are right and you are wrong. The world is divided into black and white and I know who the good guys and bad guys are. It's all figured out in my head, fortified by well-fed emotions and like-minded people." These attitudes can generate huge energy, identity, and perseverance. We sit on a pedestal of purity and false innocence. Who would want to leave—if not for a major humiliation that forces us into the pain? Paul had to be thrown to the ground and have scales fall from his eyes in order to admit that he was a self-serving Pharisee.

Denial is an understandable way of coping and surviving. It is often the only way that many people can deal with the complexity of their human situation. Sometimes when we conscientize (to arouse political consciousness) the poor or perform social analysis for the happily naïve middle class, we wonder if we are not just creating psychic problems for them. Wouldn't it be better if they did not know? Now they will only be angry and dissatisfied. That is the dangerous path of enlightenment.

The next question is more daring yet. How can I know, work through the anger, and still be a life-giving presence? Naïveté is different from second naïveté. The former is a kind of virtuous ignorance; the latter is a spirit of informed openness, often gained after disillusionment. In fact, between the two there is all the difference in the world. However, normally, we are so sure that people will not be able to work through to true enlightenment that we avoid telling them the whole truth, or they avoid wanting the whole truth. It is much, much easier *not* to know. Jesus himself understood this from the cross: "Father, forgive them, they do not know" (Luke 23:34). They really don't know! But Jesus took the harder path: to know and still forgive, and still understand.

That is the *Third Way*, beyond fight and beyond flight—and yet, in a certain sense, including both. It's fighting in a new way from within, and fleeing from the quick, egocentric response.

Only God can hold such an act together within us. The small self is always too small. Only the True Self, to which we will return later in this book, can live the gospel.

Maybe our greatest disservice has been that we have given the Law and the Gospel to the fragile self that is incapable of understanding either. We ended up condemning people to subterfuge, denial, mental gymnastics, and trivialization— *by preaching the Law without also offering people that "identity transplant" that we call the Gospel.* The Third Way is impossible, except for the True Self, "hidden with Christ in God" (Colossians 3:3). Paul took most of his Letter to the Romans to struggle with this dilemma. Law without Gospel actually paralyzes and condemns us to failure.

What Do We Do with Our Fear?

Our age has been called the age of anxiety, and I think it's probably a good description for this time. We no longer know where our foundations are. When we're not sure what is certain, when the world and our worldview keep being redefined every few months, we're going to be anxious. We want to get rid of that anxiety as quickly as we can. Yet, to be a good leader of anything today—to be a good pastor, a good bishop, or, I'm sure, a good father or mother—we have to be able to contain, to hold patiently, a certain degree of anxiety. Probably the higher the level of leader someone is, the more anxiety he or she must be capable of holding. Leaders who cannot hold anxiety will never lead us to anyplace new.

That's probably why the Bible says so often, "Do not be afraid." I have a printout showing that the phrase appears 365 times—one for each day of the year! If we cannot calmly hold a certain degree of anxiety, we will always be looking for somewhere to expel it. Expelling what we can't embrace gives us an identity, but it's a negative identity. It's not life energy, it's death energy. Formulating what we are against gives us a very quick, clear, and clean sense of ourselves. Thus, most people fall for it. People more easily define themselves by what they are against, by who they hate, by who else is wrong, instead of by what they believe in and whom they love.

I hope you see from this common pattern how different the alternative is. We might catch anew the radical and scary nature of faith, because faith only builds on that totally positive place within, however small. It needs an interior "Yes" to begin, just as the "Yes" of Mary began the entire process of salvation. God needs just a mustard-seed-sized place that is *in love*, that is open to grace, that is thrilled, that has found something wonderful. We've got to go back and build from that "Yes" place—or faith is not faith. That's why faith is always rare. Religious group-identity becomes its most common replacement. Then we don't have to find and live from a positive and loving place. We can just go to church.

It's much easier to build our identity on our group, our wounds, our angers, our agenda, our fear; that's the more normal way, unless we've been taught the way of Jesus. Almost everybody takes the easier way, because it works better in the short run. The activist might look powerful and sometimes even have a passion for social justice. But, when we draw close, sometimes we discover this isn't a person in love with God, but a person who is basically angry, oppositional, or invested in their own agenda. Maybe it's a necessary anger, but that's not yet the freedom of the gospel. Political correctness does not approach the immense gift and power of the gospel, yet educated people often confuse them. Education is not the same as transformation.

This is not to dismiss or make light of real issues of injustice. Are we to not act until we are sure that our motivation is one hundred percent pure? Should we dismiss mere humanists? Of course not! God uses all of us, with our mixed motives. We have been given, not only the conclusion, but also the way to get there. We have been shown how to fight hate without becoming hate ourselves. We have been given a Companion and a Friend, not only a good idea. We have been given joy in the midst of failure, not only a way of winning or being right. Gospel people are basically indestructible.

Some time ago, I was in Northern Ireland, where I led a series of retreats and conferences. How deeply many of the Irish people now seem to understand this Third Way! In Northern Ireland, they've lived this ping-pong game for generations, sawing the log in the same place, back and forth, with nothing new happening. The old is forever repeated. Each killing becomes a justification for another killing, and another slaughter—but now "my violence is okay because your violence was wrong."

Don't we see that there's got to be a way out of this stupidity? When both are blind, we both fall into the pit. Vengeance seems so logical, but it doesn't really work: It doesn't advance human history. The wonder of the resurrection stories in the Gospels is that Jesus has no punitive attitude toward the authorities or his cowardly followers, and that the followers themselves never call for any kind of holy war against those who killed their leader.

Something new has clearly transpired in history. This is not the common and expected story line. All Jesus does is breathe forgiveness.

It's interesting that Jesus identifies forgiveness with breathing, the one thing that we have done constantly since we were born and will do until we die. He says God's forgiveness is like breathing. Forgiveness is not apparently something God does; it is who God is. God can do no other.

An Age of Dubious Information

When I was a little Catholic boy, I thought that forgiveness was for the sake of obtaining some kind of possible or supposed moral purity and re-achieved worthiness. Now I believe that forgiveness, in the teaching of Jesus, is not for the sake of moral purity; it's quite simply for the sake of a future. There is no hope in most countries I visit. It's almost as if there is no future for this planet. Without the mystery of forgiveness and healing, we are on a straight and rather quick road toward mutual and justified destruction.

In fact, in the last forty or fifty years, we've had better scholarship, more honest history, and more access to historical records. We now can cite chapter and verse as to how and when other people have oppressed us and done us wrong. We have better knowledge than ever before as to why we have a right to our anger and our wounds. This type of progress will not create any kind of future.

I am surely happy for the honest scholarship and the access, but it is actually a two-edged sword—like all things—cutting good and cutting bad. Only wise people know how to take the information in helpful directions so we can stop victimizing in the future and not be trapped inside the resentful perspective that allows us to justify new victimizations.

René Girard wrote that, in the twentieth century, we moved scapegoating to ever-higher levels of disguise and sophistication. Without inner transformation, this is almost inevitable. Education, of itself, does not ensure we will not scapegoat. Many highly educated people still hate others, including the rich, immigrants, people of color, Jews, and Muslims, to name a few.

Is it possible that we're tearing ourselves apart, in this country, in our politics, in our churches, because there's no one out there to hate right now? We know that, even personally, we focus much better during a time of crisis. We like a clear enemy, and when the enemy is not clear, it is everywhere. Note the rise in home militias in America after the fall of the Berlin Wall.

Yet, in the supposed peace of today, fear is everywhere. The search for the appropriate enemy is rather non-stop and frantic. It seems the enemy is everywhere because the fear is unnamed and looking for a place to roost. Heads of state, once rather immune, are now the targets of choice. The litigious character of American society seems ridiculous to most of the rest of the world. Just pick up tomorrow morning's paper and see how many of the front-page articles are about one person or one group accusing someone else of being morally inferior, wrong, or some kind of "sinner." It hasn't changed since Adam scapegoated Eve and Cain killed Abel.

Anthropologically, I am told that religion begins with a distinction: the dividing of the world into the pure and the impure.

On that lie, the whole structure builds. Jesus consistently undoes historic religion by touching and consorting with and doing the "impure" things. He's not much of a founder for a self-respecting religion!

If there isn't an obvious and clear enemy, like we had during the Second World War, we normally focus on something close to home. That's why the worst and most brutal wars tend to be civil wars. That's why most murders are within the family. The deepest hatreds are often toward those inside our own group. We don't know what to do with our paranoia and hatred when there are no Communists, so now we have school violence and conspiracy theories of every sort. Look at the clear hatred between liberals and conservatives in our own churches and congress! The anger that used to safely go toward Nazis and Communists now goes toward homosexuals and abortionists in our own hometowns.

We not only remain fear-filled and hateful when we keep projecting our anxiety elsewhere, we also misdiagnose the real evil, the real problem. We normally substitute it with a smaller, closer problem that we can literally get our hands around.

Someone recently asked me why there seemed to be so many control freaks in the church. I don't think this phenomenon appears only in the church; it's everywhere. When we know we're not really transforming culture, we're not really changing the world, we're not really having a great deal of influence at the higher levels, we move to the level of micromanagement. We find some little tiny world where we can be in control and right, where we can be pure and clean. We might as well be saying, "I can't clean up the world, so at least I'm going to clean up my living room," or "I cannot really change and influence people, so I am going to demand total conformity from the pulpit."

Many of us act out some version of this. I empty all my wastebaskets. It's stupid, it doesn't make a bit of sense, but at least I feel like I am doing something. I can't change the church, but I can empty my wastebaskets and something's right inside my office. *Faith, however, allows us to hold the tension until we can recognize the true evil—of which we are a part.* That's foundational to all compassionate and nonviolent thinking.

To attack the person out there is usually to simply continue the problem, because he or she is a victim too. The reason people do evil—why they hate, sin, or make mistakes—is because at some point they have been hurt, rejected, excluded, or wounded. They just keep passing it on, and the cycle repeats and spreads. Jesus, you could say, came to break, and even stop, the cycle. Punitive behavior only continues the same old game and, I am afraid, most of the church itself has yet to understand this. We still think it is about forcing conformity instead of seeking true interior transformation. We would rather punish and coerce a response. God is much more patient.

Original Shame

What we call Original Sin in Genesis perhaps could, in a sense, be better called Original Shame, because Adam and Eve describe themselves as feeling naked. Some of the first words of God to these newly created people are, "Who told you that you were naked?" (Genesis 3:11). Next, in a lovely maternal image, God as seamstress sews leather garments for them (3:21). The first thing God does after creation itself is cover the shame of these new creatures.

This must name something that is fundamental within us. We live, not just in an age of anxiety, but also in a time of primal shame. I find very few people who do not feel inadequate, stupid, dirty, unworthy. When people come to me for counseling or confession, they always express, in one way or another, "If people only knew the things I think, the things I've done, the things I've said, the things I want to do, who would love me?" We all have that terrible feeling of a fundamental unworthiness. It takes many different forms, but somehow it appears in each of our lives.

Guilt, I am told, is about things we have done or not done, but our shame is about the primal emptiness of our very being—not what we have done, but who we are and who we are not. Guilt is a moral question. Shame—foundational shame, at least—is an ontological question. It is not resolved by changing behavior as much as by changing our very self-image, our alignment with the universe. Shame is not about what we do, but where we abide.

Nine out of ten people start with this premise: "If I behave correctly, I will one day see God clearly." Yet the biblical tradition is saying the exact opposite: If we see God clearly, we will behave in a good and human way. Our right behavior does not cumulatively lead to our true being; our true being leads to eventual right behavior. We almost all think that good morality will lead to mystical union, but, in fact, mystical union produces correct morality—along with a lot of joy left over. The greatest surprise is that, sometimes, a bad moral response is the very collapsing of the ego that leads to our falling into the hands of the living God (see Hebrews 10:31).

An Unlikely God

Christians indeed have a strange image of God: a naked, bleeding man dying on a cross. Let's be honest. If we were going to create a religion, would we ever have thought up this image of God? If I had been setting out to manufacture a religion, I would have manufactured "seven habits for highly effective people." I would have a big sun or a big golden orb for the symbol of God and I would have called God "the Force." But never in a thousand years would I have thought of an image of God as a naked, bleeding, poor man, rejected by both society and religion.

We Catholics have grown up seeing the crucifix so many times that we don't realize how off-center it is. It's not what we would think the image of God could be or should be. In fact, I don't know if we even like it. I don't know if *I* like it. It is not the way I would have preferred to think about the world. Is God eccentric here, or is it we who have not diagnosed the human situation correctly?

What question is God trying to answer by giving us a crucified man for a God? What human problem is God trying to reveal and from what is God trying to save us on the cross? We've always said that Jesus was trying to save us from our sin and, of course, that's exactly right. As Paul says, Jesus "became sin" to free us from our sin (Romans 8:3–8). What then is our "sin"?

I think it might be called "ignorant killing." Jesus reveals both the ignorance and the killing, which are both hidden from us.

Jesus receives our hatred and does not return it. He suffers and does not make the other suffer. He does not first look at changing others; he pays the price of change within himself.

He absorbs the mystery of human sin rather than passing it on. He does not use his suffering and death as power *over* others, to punish them, but as power *for* others, to transform them.

The risen Jesus is the victory fully personified. As the forgiving victim of history, he is himself transformed/resurrected and transforms/resurrects the other. He includes and forgives the sinner instead of hating the sinner and thereby continuing the pattern of hate. He gives us a history and a future beyond the predictable violence. He stops the dance toward inevitable death. He destroys death forever, as we say at Easter.

Jesus destroys the death that is eating us all alive, that is eating up our hearts. This death is our endless attempt to justify why we have a right to our hurt and to our hatred. Yet, he doesn't really cancel out death; he makes a trophy of it. It's as if he takes death and says, "Do you think you are going to use this against me, to destroy me? I'm going to use it to love you." It seems God only allows death and evil insofar as God can also use it in our favor. In the Divine Economy nothing is wasted, not even sin, evil, or death. This is God's ultimate victory.

In one sense or another, all ancient religions believed we had to spill our blood to get to God. God was distant, demanding, and dangerous. God couldn't possibly love us in our radical unworthiness. What we have in the mystery of the crucified Jesus is the reversal of all primal religion. No more human sacrifice, no more animal sacrifice, no more Jansenism (beating ourselves so we can be worthy of this God who basically doesn't like us). *Instead of our spilling blood to get to God, we have God spilling blood to get to us!* Pray on that for a week. It's enough to transform you.

God is always the initiator. God is always the Hound of Heaven,[15] going out after us because God knows our primordial shame. God is always sewing garments to cover our immense and intense sense of unworthiness. Our very movements toward God are only because God has first moved toward us. In a very true sense, Jesus undid religion forever. He was not the founder of a religion as much as he re-grounded religion in the very sin and stuff of life.

The Message of the Cross

I was teaching in the Philippines when some of this began to come together for me. I was seeing how many of the poor people there in the *barrios* still understood this cross as a message of self-punishment. Their interpretation of Christianity sometimes has a feeling of masochism to it, as if self-punishment somehow pleases God. They don't want it to be true, but they fall back into that pre-gospel thinking that we've got to spill blood to earn God's love.

Here is what I wrote in my journal while I was working on outer island:

> The message of the cross wrongly appears to most people to be passivity, heroic suffering, the cult of martyrdom, doormat theology, or refusing to fight—somehow giving up or giving in, but for God. This is very hard to change or renew in people's minds. Maybe that's why I find most people really don't believe in the message of the cross as anything practical, desirable, or even attractive. It's just something Jesus did once to resolve some necessary

heavenly metaphysical transaction, but it wasn't really an agenda for us or for now. It's something Jesus did to prove God's love for us, and we should therefore admire Jesus. That imagery is powerful, and I wouldn't want to take it away, but it's not the whole picture. The cross is about how to fight and not become casualties ourselves. The cross is about being the victory instead of just winning the victory over somebody else.

The gospel is not about winners over losers; the gospel really is about win/win—but very few get the message! I have to admit, ashamedly, that some people in the business and education worlds are better at this than some people in the church. They are beginning to understand that life cannot simply continue to be posited in terms of winners and losers. There has to be a way that we both can advance together. Mothers tend to have a head start in understanding this as a result of negotiating and compromising with their own children—whom they want to love equally and fully.

The cross is a way of winning that tries to bring along our opponent with us. The cross is refusing to hate or to humiliate the other, because that would only be to continue the same pattern and reciprocate the violence. The cross is about authentic newness. It utterly reframes the human question and forces us to redefine success. What is it we really want? What is it we're really after?

The cross is about flight, though, in the sense that we refuse the usual and predictable return punch. We flee from the predicted response so that something new and transformative can perhaps happen. We run from business as usual to reset the agenda, to reframe the question in a more positive way. It is also about fight, but with a whole new definition of what real power is and what real change is.

Traditionally, women have tended to understand this more easily than men. Men themselves have historically been victims by being put into military and business worlds where everything was framed in terms of win or lose. It kept them in the dualistic mindset much longer. The competitive paradigm became the only way that many men knew how to read reality. They thought that to be a hero meant to win. What the cross was supposed to do for Christians was redefine the true hero and heroine forever. In the first two thousand years, only a small minority of clerics or laity ever got the point. Most of us continued in the old punitive system and, in fact, continued the same story line. By that time, it was in our hard wiring.

The cross is how to work for the answer without becoming part of the problem itself. Look to any number of wars to see why this is right. Even in the struggles of third-world revolutions, we see, again and again, that people search for some kind of economic reform through fighting and the use of power. Invariably, when the revolutionaries get into positions of power, they do the same thing that had been done before. Most revolutions begin on the left of the political spectrum and end on the right. This movement is inevitable if the self is not transformed. If the self is not transformed, then it was not really the journey into powerlessness, the mystery of the cross, that inspired the revolution. It was simply another form of dominative power. Jesus is, in some ways, the only true revolutionary. Most revolutions merely rearrange the furniture on the deck of the *Titanic*. Jesus built a new boat.

Unless spirituality answers the questions of power and powerlessness, there is never any real reform. There is never any real advancement in human history, because the so-called reformers are done in by the struggle. *The cross is finally about how to stand against hate without becoming hate ourselves.*

How can we stand against hate without letting it frame the question? Isn't that the fundamental question for all of us? How do we oppose the evil, the hurts, the betrayals, the abandonment, the rejections, the disappointments in our lives, the people who let us down, the people who turn against us, the people who tell lies about us? How do we stand against that without becoming a mirror image of the same thing?

The human capacity to hate and kill is *the sin* of the world and it took a Lamb (see John 1:29) to dismantle what the lions of history could only perpetuate.

Saint Bonaventure's Coincidence of Opposites

The cross is an image onto which we can hold and from which we can draw life. It is a visual metaphor for the paradoxical nature of all things. The cross is saying that there is *a cruciform pattern to reality*. Reality is not meaningless and absurd (chaos/no patterns/nihilism), but neither is it perfect consistency (rationalism/scientism/fundamentalism). Reality, rather, is filled with contradictions. That's why the medieval Franciscan Saint Bonaventure (1221–1274), and others, called it "the coincidence of opposites."[16] Jesus was killed on the collision of cross-purposes, conflicting interests, and half-truths that is all of life. The cross was the price that Jesus paid for agreeing to live in a "mixed" world that was both human and divine, bad and good, simultaneously broken and utterly whole. He agreed to carry the mystery and not to demand perfection of God's creation or of God's creatures. He lived fully on the horns of the human dilemma and made it work for us. In fact, he said it is the *only* way. It is in that sense only that Christianity is the "only" way to be saved. We are, indeed, saved by the cross—more than we realized.

Experience of the cruciform pattern of reality always feels like two steps forward and three steps backward. None of us likes it, especially because the three steps backward always feel like dying. Many of us working in the church right now feel we're in a period of moving three steps backward—a period of dying. Yet Jesus shows us on the cross that this is the only and constant pattern, and we should not be shocked or surprised by it. The people who *live the contradictions*, in fact, are the saviors of the world. These are the people who are the agents of all true transformation, reconciliation, and newness.

People will think that we're asking them to compromise on issues or on truth if we talk this way. They will call us moral relativists or something that sounds dangerous, which seems to be what they thought of Jesus. I want to say this very strongly: That's a smoke screen. That's a diversionary tactic, even if unintentional. This labeling is a way to avoid the horns of the dilemma, to deny the clearly paradoxical nature of almost everything.

We are so hesitant to live with the scandal of particularity, which is the primary pattern in the biblical revelation. As soon as we start to discern a clear pattern, the Bible makes an exception to it. I'm not talking about compromising on issues, because I do think society has to decide what is acceptable behavior and what is not. I'm talking about compromising on ego, which nobody wants to do. People say they do not want to give way on important moral issues, but far too often they don't want to give way on the ego's need to be right, superior, and in control. This mimics that original sin, described as a "desire to be like God" and daring to eat the apple of the tree of the knowledge of good and evil. It's the human unwillingness to live in a broken world. In the illusion of an unbroken world, we do not have to rely upon grace, mercy, and forgiveness. We do not need to be "saved."

Yet, if God does not make exceptions, all of us are in trouble. The evil people I've met in my fifty years of priesthood are always absolutely certain they're right. They suffer no self-doubt. They are certain they have the whole truth. Fortunately, I've been blessed to meet many holy people too. When we meet a holy person, there is a very different aroma, a very different energy, a very different taste and smell. They want to do God's will. They seek to please God, but, like Thomas Merton (1915–1968) at the end of his life, they are saying, "the fact that I think I am following your will does not mean that I am actually doing so. But I believe that the desire to please you does in fact please you."[17] That very desire is itself a gift of God. There is not much to brag about in being human!

Who among us can say with total certitude that we know we're doing God's will? I can't, any day of my life, and it's very unsatisfying. That's what it means to bear the mystery, to hang with Jesus on the horns of the human dilemma, to agree to find God in a clearly imperfect world. We would much sooner have certitudes, we would much sooner have order and control and know who the good guys and the bad guys are. We don't want to hang in this ambiguous, compromised place with Jesus. Most prefer dogma and perfectly objective morality to biblical faith any day. Certitude allows us to predict and control outcomes, and to justify rewards and punishments. That's not all bad. The trouble is that it is not the message that shouts from the cross.

Liberals and Conservatives

The more progressive and liberal type of person tends to avoid what I'll call the vertical claims of the gospel. They tend to be afraid to talk about transcendence and God. They tend to be uncomfortable talking about the wisdom and the importance of the past and of tradition, to know that the truth has always been with us and God has always been with us. Progressive and educated people often love right ideas more than reality in its wounded state. We could call that the vertical line of the cross: transcendence and tradition.

Conservative people tend to avoid the horizontal claims of the gospel. They tend to be afraid of breadth and inclusiveness. They tend to be afraid of mercy and compassion, or any breaking of the rules, particularly rules for group coherence. It's almost as if letting the sinner get in will take away their purity and their worthiness or the identity of their group. They are always circling the wagons around this very fragile God that they have to protect. Often, their religion is more about tribalism and group belonging rather than any real search for broad truth.

Group belonging takes away a lot of primal shame and fear for most of us.

The liberal types fight structures, authority, and self-serving ideologies, not realizing that they usually become very individualistic and heady as a result. The liberal types also play the victim whenever it is politically correct to do so. They have a very hard time creating anything that lasts because they are loyal to so little beyond their own experience and their own agenda. Authority is always suspect, and we cannot build positively when we start with suspicion. They also do not pass on their values very well to their children, probably because their values are more against-energy than for-energy. Against-energy does not inspire or convert young, idealistic people. Political correctness gathers very few, and only for a very short time.

The conservative types fight as soon as they have targeted the appropriate sinner, or anyone who threatens their strong control needs. These people expel and reject rather readily, very often creating scapegoats, which take away their own self-doubt. There is often a pseudo innocence in conservative people, which naturally comes from refusing to carry the shadow side of reality. This refusal leads to a false moral superiority and a naïve certitude, which we call fundamentalism. Conservative types tend to flee from inclusiveness, from depth, and from much-needed self-knowledge. They usually have a strong punitive need, perhaps to restore an appropriate sense of an ordered world. There are no free lunches for most conservatives, while liberals are always looking for one, for themselves or others.

Together, though, we hang, each with our own needs for conversion. Wherever we find ourselves on the spectrum, we hope we have part of the truth and part of the mystery. The cross calls all of us to a mystery of transformation. On the cross, none of us is in charge, none of us is in control, and none of us can possibly understand, just like Jesus himself. On the cross, someone else is in control. Someone else is in charge. Someone else understands. Someone else is obviously a much more patient lover than we are.

Three

Great Awakenings

Students of history know that our current thirst for transcendence is not the first such American experience. The United States has seen three spiritual awakenings. These were widespread religious awakenings, or revivals. These awakenings can be criticized on some levels, but they produced a model of social justice and human rights that is still copied worldwide. The first, which historians call The Great Awakening, carried the seeds of the American Revolution, the United States Constitution, and, ultimately, the French Revolution. Human consciousness and freedoms made a great advance from which we have never withdrawn, at least in principle. The Great Awakening contributed to the modern democratic worldview, the French Declaration of the Rights of Man and of the Citizen, and the concern for the common person. It laid the foundation for the rights of women and minorities.

The Second Great Awakening, which began at the turn of the nineteenth century, contributed to the eventual abolition of slavery. It was almost as if freedom and human dignity were ideas whose time had come. The soul and the spirit had to be ready for the movement of history. The Second Great Awakening, by calling people to reflect on a transcendent reference point, helped pave the way for a higher morality than mere cultural expedience.

Although most find slavery unthinkable now, it is worth re-membering that, in much of colonial America, it was assumed that the institution of slavery was embedded in the only way the world had ever been structured. Even in the Bible, Paul assumed that the institution of slavery was normal—a good example of how we cannot normally think outside of our own era and culture. Human consciousness has only slowly been ready for the full Christ, for the freedom of the children of God. No surprise that it took us until the 1980s to begin to see the evil of sexism!

The assumption of the necessity of slavery is true even of the very progressive American Constitution, which, as we all know, was written by *white* men with *men* in mind, because women did not have the vote and black men were slaves. Our founding fathers were well-intentioned and brilliant rationalists, but truly blinded by their own time and culture. We also are blinded by our time and culture, and we cannot yet see it. Surely this is a strong example of how education is not the same as transforma-tion, a theme I will continue to emphasize.

The mind can only take pictures using the film with which it's been loaded. Our inner myths determine what we do and don't notice, what we consider significant and what we ignore. If we had had the openness of ears to hear the full gospel, we would have had the openness of eyes to see that slavery and sexism were significant. But our eyes were not ready yet, nor maybe our heart—nor was history.

In the wake of the second spiritual awakening, Abraham Lincoln (1809–1865) emerged and grew into his greatness. He wasn't always an emancipator, by the way. There must have come an epiphanic moment when he first saw slavery as intolerable.

The great souls get there first, eventually they filter down to intermediate souls (most of us), and it takes much longer to get to those who are either uninformed or afraid.

Those who think that the world can only be structured as *they* have known it are the slow learners of history. They fail to realize that their slow learning curve is actually a form of narcissism and also a lack of knowledge. Thus, change comes with great difficulty in human history. God seems to rely on the first group of "great souls" to call the rest of us forward, inch by inch, and they normally suffer a great deal for their foreseeing. Most of us like our comfort zones and take them for granted, as we once took for granted the divine right of kings.

The Lincolns of this world are people who have experienced what the New Testament writers termed *metanoia*. The word literally means "a turnaround." It is a fundamental transformation of mind, normally brought about by personal suffering, great awareness, or Damascus Road experiences. This reveals an utterly new imaginal world. Until we "imagine" our worldview differently, intellect and will, of themselves, provide only temporary and often weak change. *Metanoia*, an utter turnaround, involves seeing with a new mind and is seemingly necessary to transform us personally and to help us transform social structures and institutions. In other words, we are, first of all, *assumed* to be on a course of ego, narcissism, and self-interest, with a what's-in-it-for-me attitude.

Other disciplines might speak of "insight," "eureka moments," "flow," or "peak experiences," but *metanoia* is always known to be a grace from nowhere. The recipients always know for sure that it is an utterly unearned gift. If they don't, they are destroyed by their own *hubris*, or pride. The biblical tradition would say that this turnaround is entirely dependent upon an experience of The Absolute. Afterward, we know at least three things at a deep level: God is good, the world is good, and I am good. That is all we need in order to begin. We then have an utterly grounded imaginal consciousness, and fear has been foundationally overcome. Our psyche is no longer based in the small self, but in the Great Self, the Christ Self.

People like Lincoln, Harriet Tubman (c. 1822–1913), and some abolitionists represented this second awakening. It is embarrassing how absent the voices of mainline churches were during this period. Catholics were still building separate churches for blacks and whites into the early 1960s in some parts of the South. Claims to orthodoxy become very weak when there is almost no orthopraxy.

The third awakening was not so long ago. It was the stirring that led to the labor and civil-rights reforms of the mid-twentieth century. It predisposed American Catholics for the reforms that would come with the Second Vatican Council (1962–1965). It gave us the beginnings of what I call "the bias toward the bottom." We can only realize how significantly our thinking has changed back to biblical thinking (where the victims were always the heroes) when we remember that most of human history has idealized kings, money, nobility, fame, and power (the bias toward the top).

The Security to Be Insecure

At the time of the Second Vatican Council, we Catholics were very self-confident. All indicators of numbers, vocations, money, and influence were positive and growing. There was no reason to reform or self-criticize. Our identity was clear, our boundaries were clear, our sense of the absolute was grounded and founded. We knew who we were and, ironically, we were therefore free to criticize ourselves, even from the very top.

The ability to self-criticize and own our shadow side is a clear sign of health and interior freedom. A historian of social change once told me that Vatican II was one of the very few times in all of human history that a strong institution reformed itself from the top—when it didn't have to and wasn't forced to. That's a rather strong sign of the presence of God's Spirit.

Before Cardinal Jorge Mario Bergoglio was elected pope in 2013 and took the name Pope Francis I, the Roman Church, at the higher levels, had little ability to be self-critical. We felt that we had lost our boundaries in relation to secular culture, and we were trying to reinforce them by insisting that we were always right and had the full and total picture. This is called a "siege mentality," which always emerges when a group has lost its former influence and feels that it is under attack.

We are all caught in these bigger *zeitgeists* ("the spirit of an age"). Every age has been. It is almost heroic to live above them, and we never really know if we are doing so. Yet, the person with a great soul can move others toward the future with compassion and confidence—not judgment, paranoia, or accusation. We were very happy as Catholics when John Paul II (1920–2005) set a new tone in Jubilee Year 2000 and publicly admitted and asked forgiveness for many of the historic sins of Roman Catholicism. It seemed to give permission at all lower levels for honesty and humility about the Church.

John Paul II was surely one of these great souls on many levels. His tragic flaw might well be that he did not often trust anyone else to be a great soul or to initiate the grand gesture except himself. He could be ecumenical, but we at the lower levels had to exclude even other Christians from the table. He could make major political statements, but other bishops and priests, like the martyr Saint Óscar Romero (1917–1980), were given no support when they did the same. It felt a bit schizophrenic, but the issues are so enormous today that only time will prove where wisdom lies (see Matthew 11:19).

Finger-pointing is usually just an avoidance of our own transformation. To continue to move forward calmly, with joy and confidence, is probably as clear a sign of God's presence as I can imagine. It is also somewhat rare, but those, like Pope Francis, who can do so are the people who will reconstruct. These are the people who will lead us into God's future. These are the people to whom it is worth listening.

Dom Hélder Câmara (1909–1999), the Archbishop of Recife in Brazil, continued to live and preach with joy and confidence, even after his human rights programs were discontinued by a later Vatican appointment. Most women foundresses of religious communities spent much of their life being opposed by bishops and Roman congregations, yet they humbly moved forward with what they knew God had called them to do. These kinds of fire-tried saints will always win the day for God.

A Sense of History

One of the greatest qualities we must bring to the present malaise, the present dilemma, is a sense of history, a sense that we've been here before. We've seen the overly romantic and the overly rational before. Those extremes have been interwoven throughout history. During the best of times, they've balanced each other. We're not in that balance now. We're either cheaply romantic (most media and liberals), or cheaply rational (many conservatives and fundamentalist religions). We're not open, by and large, to great spirituality or to dealing with things holistically and historically. We just react.

Healthy religion—which profits both the individual and the society—will be both romance *and* reason, faith *and* intelligence, symbol *and* science, experience *and* essence. In Richard Tarnas' masterful overview of Western thought, *The Passion of the Western Mind*,[18] he describes our entire history of philosophy as a balancing act, a pendulum swing between the rational and the romantic. Seldom does it achieve a balance between the two.

Strangely enough, the present liberal-conservative split in the Catholic Church is a mishmash of both on both sides. Conservatives romantically hold onto essence while being very rational about experience; liberals rationally hold onto experience while being very romantic about essence. That tells me they both have a kind of truth and wholeness. However, they are each usually incapable of self-criticism or of appreciating the other.

Yet, in the midst of this confusion, people of true greatness are emerging, probably sometimes *because* of the confusion and chaos. As always, the Spirit cannot be controlled and "blows where it pleases" (John 3:8). Jesus is just too much for any one group of us. How good it is to accept that. What a burden off our backs, our judgments, our inflated expectations of everything. Now only God needs to be God.

Many of our social institutions, particularly government, law, education, the church, the military, family, and marriage have been roundly discredited in the last seventy years. Each one is its own sad story of lost authority and focus. Unfortunately, this leaves only the media and the business world to communicate daily meaning for most people. That is scary—and this is probably the first time in human history that we have tried to carry society on two such tiny and fragile shoulders. It is certain to produce fragile people and a very unstable society.

Many feel that the traditional institutions of our culture are impotent and incapable of communicating believable patterns of wisdom and truth. Lacking authority and credibility, they do not have the power to lead or guide us. We don't give power to them, and they don't have the consensus or the confidence to take it. The wars in Iraq and Afghanistan and the scandals of the Trump presidency have made us cynical about government and politics. Recent racially charged trials have made us cynical about the legal-judiciary system. Both Catholic and Evangelical fundamentalism, plus the sexual scandals of the clergy, have made us cynical about religion. Our universities do not make us into universal people, but instead have become mostly job-preparation mills that leave students in debt for most of their careers. At the personal level, our individualism and narcissism have made the skills needed for marriage and family rare.

This power and confidence vacuum has opened the door for the far right to seize and exploit the language of religion and God. The televangelist phenomenon, within both Evangelical Protestantism and pious Catholicism, is in great part, I believe, the fault of the liberal establishment in this country, which refuses even to acknowledge transcendence or tradition in any serious way, forcing an overreaction on the other side. Both sides righteously point to the opposite's extremes to justify their own positions. True greatness never emerges in such periods, I am told. We spend too much time putting out fires, attacking, and protecting ourselves to focus on intelligence and mysticism. What is lost is the healthy middle, where the romantic and the rational can coexist—and that is a big loss.

When we take an extreme position, we take part of the responsibility for pushing people to the opposite extreme. I see, for example, in my own small world, many young priests, laity, and new bishops with whom I find it very hard to relate. They seem to me rather rigid, ideological, and doctrinaire. Yet, when I talk to them personally, I can see them living in fear of the judgments of the feminists and the attacks of the liberals. I can see that they have been hurt by such attacks. We all go to a place where we can feel safe.

When we do not feel safe or secure or "at home," we naturally take a strong stance to defend ourselves. Unfortunately, that puts us in a corner that we cannot escape and where others cannot get to us. That's not a very good position from which to proclaim the great Good News. Of course, conservatives push progressives to the same reactionary position by their seeming worship of authority and order as ends in themselves. To educated people, most traditionalists appear to have no interest in honest history or critical thinking, but only in soft piety and propaganda passing for religion. So the liberals get out their information, statistics, and scholarship and use them to dismiss the conservatives as promoters of romantic rubbish. The trouble is that both are, to some extent, right.

Stephen Carter makes the point that the liberal establishment in America must recognize that it has unwittingly allowed for the ascendancy of the far right through its own nihilism, its throwing out of all boundary markers, its thinking that history began yesterday with us, and its stomping on necessary traditions and "romantic" rituals. Progressive folks have been far too rational and politically "correct" about the needs of the soul.

Can we take responsibility for the fact that we push people to such extremes when we do not stand in the compassionate middle? I think of how often, during my talks, someone raises a hand and says, "I disagree with what you just said." Eight times out of ten, they did not hear what I said. Normally, they don't have the humility to ask, in a non-accusatory way: "Did I hear you correctly in saying . . . ?" or "What do you mean when you say . . . ?" The assumption is seldom that *they* could have heard me wrong. The assumption is usually that *I* am wrong. Such a mentality never encourages dialogue or mutuality. Unfortunately, my response too often suffers because of the negative energy generated. I am then defensive or bite my tongue to control my own judgments or desire to attack back. The result is a half response, at best, because the environment is not safe and congenial.

Our assumption is usually: "I did understand you. I know your motivation. I know what you're trying to say, and I therefore have the need and right to attack you." Normally, neither of us grows or expands in such a context. The truth is not well served, because neither of us feels secure or respected. Unfortunately, this has become the state of our public discourse, even in places like the senate and among major editorial writers. I wonder if we in the church have shown them a viable alternative.

Fortunately, there will always be the two out of ten people who have the humility to ask, "Richard, did I understand what you were saying?" Normally then I can clarify, or perhaps admit that I have communicated poorly or am, in fact, incorrect. I normally tell people to "listen long enough to me and you won't get too upset." I'll usually balance myself out if they give me enough time, but a lot of people will not give each other enough time.

In hostile situations, we find that Jesus either kept silent, reframed the question, or put a question back to the speaker. He knew that we never win when someone has a predisposition toward resentment or a desire to shame us. In such encounters, whatever we say will be turned against us. We have all been in such fruitless and impossible conversations. No one wins.

But that is the way the ego likes to work. Opposition gives us a sense of standing for something, a false sense of control and power. Compassion and humility don't give us a sense of control or psychic comfort. We have to let go of our moral high ground and hear the ten percent of truth that the other person is perhaps telling. Compassion and dialogue are essentially vulnerable positions. If we are into control and predictability, we will seldom descend into the weakness of listening or the scariness of dialogue. We will not only be incapable of hearing others, but will also be incapable of hearing God. *How we do anything is how we do everything.* If we spend all day controlling and blocking others, why would we change when we kneel to pray?

Faith, frankly, demands *faith*—not proof, certitude, predictability, control, or the comforts of authority assuring us that we are always right. Our temptation is often to create a non-relational Christianity and non-relational leadership styles, so we can have all the bases covered by custom and statute, and don't ever have to enter into the scandal of particularity. Prayer, perhaps more than anything, is the school of relationship and particularity. We should be the experts in these areas—if we are people of prayer.

A Sense of Community

The hunger for meaning and the need for hope in this deconstructed society cannot be satisfied by merely private choices. This is a real blind spot for most liberals. The issues are too big and we cannot stand alone against such a dominant cultural collapse. Corporate evil can only be overcome by corporate good. For this reason, and many others, I'm very happy to see the growth of small groups in church and in society.

As I have said since the early days of the New Jerusalem Community in Cincinnati, *we cannot think ourselves into a new way of living; we must live ourselves into a new way of thinking.* It is lifestyle choices that finally change us and allow us to see in new ways. We have to create structures and institutions that think, and therefore act, differently. We have no past evidence to prove that gospel individuals *alone* can fully exemplify the Reign of God. This is the church's own form of individualism, while it often condemns individualism in the world. Until we question our very lifestyle, nothing truly new is going to happen—or, as Jesus said in a perfect metaphor, if we put "new wine into old wineskins," both will be lost (see Mark 2:22). That's a rather clear statement about the need for gospel structures to support gospel individuals. Up to now, we have largely tried to evangelize individuals while the structures have remained monarchical and unaccountable. "Put new wine in fresh wineskins, and both are preserved" (Matthew 9:17).

Perhaps that is why Jesus does not directly take on social reform. Instead, he preaches a life of simplicity and nonviolence that is simply *outside* the system of power, money, and control. More than directly fighting the system, *he ignores it* and builds an alternative worldview where power, prestige, and possessions are not sought or even admired. Such withdrawal of allegiance is finally the most subversive act possible because the powers that be can no longer control us, either positively or negatively (by getting us to react against them). We are no longer inside their reward-and-punishment system. Maybe that is why mystics, saints, and hermits so infuriate the body politic. They ignore the whole thing and build an alternative set of loyalties.

Good Tradition

My brother and sister-in-law similarly set their family outside the mainstream. They purchased a house on the same street as her family and committed to sharing a Catholic worldview, saying, "We are going to raise our kids with a different set of values." When I saw my nephews and their cousins together, I said, "They are different; they really are different." They brought their dogs over for me to bless them. They had no embarrassment in talking about church or even in calling me "Father."

Now, some would have said this was old-fashioned and patriarchal, but when I saw that the alternative was cynicism and sarcasm about almost everything, a calm world of mutual respect started looking rather beautiful. They were proud of being Catholic. They carried none of the shame that many young Catholic kids had. They were so excited that a priest was visiting, so I was blessing animals and sick people all week! For these folks, it was still an enchanted universe, filled with communion and mystery. If religion does not give us that sense of belonging to a sacred world of meaning, it is rather useless. If we see the world as blessed, then we want our pets in on it too!

While staying at my brother's house, I observed a world where voices were rarely raised and where the parents and children spoke to one another with mutual respect. I didn't think we sophisticated folks needed to assume that they were all repressed and "in denial." The people I meet who are not cynical are normally people who hold more conservative values—or progressive people who also have a deep spirituality. They are still proud of being whatever they are, and do not waste most of their lives debunking the only life they have. There are always some stable *givens* in their lives, and they do not need to hold them up for daily critique.

Perhaps, like my brother and sister-in-law, they wouldn't think of missing Mass on Sunday. The sacramental symbols and the feast days of the Church are an active part of their life and their week. This gave the children, especially, a sacred and safe world within which they could grow—almost endlessly and almost effortlessly. I know this because I had such a world myself, in somewhere-over-the-rainbow Kansas, where I grew up in those safe, idyllic years after the Second World War. Ironically, this prepared me for a world much larger than Kansas. What a paradox!

It seems we must *begin* conservatively—with clear boundaries, identity, and a sense of respect for our reality. Then, and only then, can we move out from that strong center, according to our education and experience. I really do not know any other way that works for the human soul. We cannot begin by being aimless, reactionary, and picking up pieces on our own. If we do, we have the extreme handicap of beginning at *zero*, which I don't think God ever intended for the individual. That's the necessary and good meaning of Tradition. We were meant to be parts of communities of custom, where some of the problems have already been named and resolved for us, even if we still have to do it our own way.

The normal pattern that I find in mythology and story is that the healthy person always begins with idealism, heroism, and black-and-white worldviews, and then moves toward nuance, compassion, exception, patience, tolerance, and wisdom. We now have it backward: People begin with no boundaries or identity and then overreact by the middle of life and need all kinds of fundamentalist certitudes, clarity, order, and absolute authority! I saw this especially at the jail where I ministered, with many who wasted their early years on "drugs, sex, and rock and roll," and then fought about religious platitudes with absolute arrogance and ignorance—a toxic combination! This is probably predictable for many baby boomers and later generations. It does not bode well for the future of religion, or even for the future of intelligent conversation.

To live with healthy Tradition is not an individual experience—it is a communal one. Perhaps this is why Catholicism emphasizes liturgy so much. It is the one thing that pulls us into a communal space where we can ask different questions, look at reality from a different perspective, and be told different truths, beyond the small truths of the private "I." The endless telling of "this is me" stories eventually becomes self-validating, self-imprisoning, and, frankly, boring. Personal anecdotes become too small and aimless, unless they are a part of some larger life narratives. That is the genius of family stories, mythologies, and the biblical mind.

Reconstruction

When we speak of rebuilding, we're talking in great part about the rebuilding of a public world, public institutions, and public forums. Attitudinal change is only a beginning, and still too privatized. We start with personal conversion, but then we must move toward structures that can allow that vision to be shared with other people and to be passed on to the next generation. As I said before, conservative people tend to be better at this than progressives, who build few lasting structures. This is probably why most religion is inherently conservative. The genius is to distinguish between healthy conservatism and mere self-serving maintenance of status-quo structures. People can look conservative and merely be afraid of larger truth, imagination, intelligence, risk, and, finally, faith. God deserves more than that. True traditionalists are not always conservative by temperament. True traditionalists just know that there are some old boundary markers that were put there for a reason.

Ralph Waldo Emerson (1803–1882), the great American essayist, said "nothing great is ever achieved without enthusiasm."[19] What a deconstructed culture lacks, because of its deep cynicism and pessimism about reality, is a basic confidence and enthusiasm that is necessary to start almost anything. We cannot begin with mere criticism or againstness—or it finally turns against our own group (witness the later stages of most angry revolutions, even much of the work of the *Protest*ant Reformation, and the new Catholic reactionaries who are already splitting over who is more orthodox). The brittle or negative personality finally breaks against itself and its own type. We can only build on life, not on death.

I will always cherish my early years among the youth of the New Jerusalem Community in Cincinnati. If we were nothing else, we were enthusiastic! There was belief, there was trust, there was positive energy—everything was not immediately critiqued, analyzed, and called into question. I always said, "Let's be free to say 'yes' before we say 'no.'" Over the years, my appreciation for the profoundness of that truth has deepened. The Alcoholics Anonymous saying that "analysis is paralysis" indicates a learned pattern that many educated people need to unlearn.

Most of us are not free to say "yes" before we say "no." Our first response is normally "no": "I don't trust that. I don't like that. I don't agree with that." The word *enthusiasm* (*en-theos* in Greek) means "filled with God." I'm not encouraging mindless enthusiasm, but the enthusiasm that is based on intelligence, wisdom, and the great gift of hope. Hope is a participation in the very life of God. This hope has nothing to do with circumstances or events going well. It can even thrive in adversity and trial. True faith, which always includes hope and love, is a predisposition to "yes." I would say that a foundational "yes" is the most distinguishing element between a secular agenda and one that is guided by the Spirit of Jesus. You can spot the different energy in a moment! "With him it was always 'yes,' and however many the promises God made, the 'yes' to them all is in him" (2 Corinthians 1:19b–20). Jesus was a "yes" man in the deepest meaning of that phrase.

If you were to come to our Center for Action and Contemplation in New Mexico and saw the staff walking around badmouthing others, or frenetically pushing for their own agenda, you would not think much of us. You would not believe that we were representing the new agenda of God and calling forth a Greater Truth—and you would be right. When we are doing "God's thing," we don't need to push the river. The river is God's unilateral and always-reliable love. That should make our style, even our corporate style, utterly different than that of almost anybody else. We can be positive and even cheerful because it does not all depend on our getting it right or doing it right. We are merely, as Francis said, "a servant of the Great King."[20]

Stringing Pearls

Once we are critical or educated people, deconstructionism will come naturally to most of us. For some reason, "no" comes more easily than "yes," and is almost the very proof that we are indeed sophisticated. But deconstruction is rather useless without reconstruction, without a positive vision. As I said in Chapter Two, it is the easiest thing in the world to point out what is wrong, who is wrong, and to stand on a pedestal of superiority—without *doing* anything positive or *becoming a positive answer* ourselves. After we deconstruct, what are we actually *for*? An awful lot of activists on the left and reactionaries on the right have no positive vision, nothing they believe *in*, no one they are in love *with*.

They are just overwhelmed with what's wrong and think that by eliminating the so-called "contaminating element," the world will be pure and right again.

That is the major illusion of people on both left and right. In different ways, they are both into a politics of expulsion. It's just the object of their expulsion that is different. One day, the mainline Christian movement will itself recognize that Jesus was never into expelling or excluding—only transforming and integrating. In fact, you might say that, for Jesus, the very act of expulsion is the problem. He is always sending the lepers and those healed back into the city, back to the priests, out of the cemetery of chains and gnashing of teeth.

We're glad that people are working for justice and peace. We are happy that people are seeking to overcome evil. But problem-solving, punishing offenders, and shunning the non-conformists will not, of itself, create a new vision, a new society. Without a positive vision, the Book of Proverbs says, the people will perish (see 29:18). What the gospel, what true religion, what true mythology gives us is a cosmic and positive vision, inside of which the soul can live safely. That's the only place from which lasting change ever comes. Jesus's term for that totally positive vision—not against anybody or expelling anything—is the Reign of God. He *includes* (forgives) sinners instead of excluding or scapegoating them. In that light, it is rather amazing that institutional Christianity ever created the very concept of excommunication. Only the individual can do that to him- or herself, and we had best not make it our corporate concern. Hinduism, the oldest religion in the world, has never excommunicated anybody.

"Garbage in, garbage out," the healing professions have been saying. Some people call this phenomenon karma or define it as meaning, "What we give out is what we will get back." If we build on death, we end up with death. If we build on life, we end up with more of the same, because spiritual gifts increase with usage. A Hasidic master put it best of all: "Rake the muck this way, rake the muck that way—it will still be muck... In the time I am brooding over it I could be stringing pearls for the delight of Heaven."[21]

I once heard the German theologian Dorothee Sölle (1929–2003) speak. Per my notes, she said we are spiritual orphans in the West today, having lost access to our own spiritual roots, which are the only ones that we have. She's right: The young people of Germany, she said, travel the world to find their own spiritual heritage. They can't find it at home anymore because everybody has rejected their own tradition after it failed them so miserably in the Nazi era.

Aleksandr Solzhenitsyn (1918–2008), the Russian writer, put it even more desperately when he wrote, "the Western system in its present state of spiritual exhaustion does not look attractive."[22] It's a telling metaphor. The Western mind refuses to be in awe anymore. It is only aware of what is wrong, and seemingly incapable of rejoicing in what is still good and true. The only way out is through a new imagination and new cosmology, created by positive God-experience. Education, liberal politics, problem-solving, and rigid ideology are all finally inadequate by themselves to create cosmic hope and meaning. Only great religion can do that, which is probably why Jesus spent so much of his ministry trying to reform religion. Nothing less will do.

Healthy religion gives us a foundational sense of awe. It re-enchants an otherwise empty universe. It gives people a universal reverence toward all things. Only with such reverence do we find confidence and coherence. Only then does the world become a safe home. Then we can see the reflection of the divine image in the human, in the animal, in the entire natural world—which has now become inherently "supernatural." That is the paradox, and all dualistic language will henceforth fail us. When the divine image is no longer present, why should I respect you, or anything? Why should I talk to you with tenderness if you do not reflect the divine image, if you are just another market product?

Humanism is actually a result of the gospel, but it is not the gospel itself, because it refuses the total seeing and foundation for absolute reverence. It tries to obey the second commandment without the first, and therefore is finally inadequate. (Although we must admit that many humanists seem to love their neighbor in practice much better than many professed Christians. God uses all of us as instruments. Christians just have the advantage of knowing they are indeed instruments—and living in that joy now.)

It is, of course, finally the doctrine of the cross which pushes this divine reflection to its utter limits. More than anything else, the cross says that God can and must be seen in all things, but most especially in the seemingly sinful, broken, and tragic things. The place of the supposed worst becomes the place of the very best. The mystery of the cross teaches us to be prepared to be surprised about how and where God reveals God's heart. It is beyond our control.

The Sacred Wound

When we lose the reflection of the divine image in all things, we quickly disintegrate. The postmodern mind has too little respect (*re-spicere*, "to look again"), too little ability to look again at what it has too easily dismissed. Both superficial science and much secular education have limited themselves to only partial seeing.[23] With too little respect, the postmodern mind won't see all the way through things. It's the same with a lot of therapy and psychology: They're right, as far as they go, but they stop too soon. Healthy religion pushes us all the way through. It tells us, "Don't stop with your anger, your disillusionment, your scientific explanation." Deconstruction is only the first stage toward a new reconstruction. The biblical prophets would have called it "the toppling of idols," which rightly precedes the entrance into the temple of the true sacred.

Christianity, in its mature forms, keeps pushing us toward the necessary tragic: "the folly of the cross," as Paul calls it (1 Corinthians 1:18).

Normally, the way God pushes us is by disillusioning us with the present mode. Until the present falls apart, we will never look for something more. We will never discover what it is that really sustains us. That dreaded falling-apart experience is always suffering in some form. All of us hate suffering, yet all religions talk about it as necessary. It seems to be the price we pay for the death of the small self and the emergence of the True Self, when we finally come to terms with our true identity in God. Many Jungians describe this in psychological terms as the "necessary soul suffering" that comes from the death of the ego. Jesus would say, "Unless the grain of wheat dies, it remains just a grain of wheat" (John 12:24). By avoiding this legitimate pain of being human, we sadly bring on ourselves much longer lasting and, often, fruitless pain.

In our men's spirituality work, we call that suffering, in its transformed state, "the sacred wound," a concept drawn from classical mythology, but also from the Christ story. In mythology, the would-be hero is always wounded. The word *innocent* (*innocens*, "not yet wounded") is not a complimentary term in mythology. The *puer* is the young boy who refuses to be wounded, or, more exactly, refuses to recognize and suffer the wounds that are already there. He's just going to remain nice and normal, so everybody will accept him. In our culture, he might smugly remain white and middle class, healthy, "sinless," Catholic, pretty, and happy, maybe even drive a classy car or wear the latest clothing. He refuses to let things fall apart. He refuses to be wounded, much less to allow the humiliating wound to become sacred and sanctifying. Yet, I personally believe that the Gospels are saying there is no other way to know something essential. Allowing our always-unjust wounds to, in fact, become sacred wounds, is the unique Christian name for salvation. *We always learn our mystery at the price of our innocence.*

Now, if we can trust the pain, and not get rid of it until we have learned its lessons, the suffering can be seen as a part of the great pattern of how God is transforming all things. If there is one consistent and clear revelation in the Judeo-Christian Scriptures, it is that the God of Israel is the one who *turns death into life* (see Deuteronomy 32:39, Romans 4:17, 2 Corinthians 1:9). When we can trust the transformative pattern, when we can trust that God is *in the suffering*, our wounds become sacred wounds and the actual and ordinary life journey becomes itself the godly journey, trusting God to be in all things, especially in sin and suffering.

Catholics reaffirm this unwelcome truth at the heart of every eucharistic liturgy, knowing how easy it is to forget *the* mystery of faith. Let me personalize it and paraphrase it in this way: *Christ and the soul must die. Christ and the soul must rise. That pattern must happen many times before we understand it.*

Paul states this even more clearly in Galatians (2:19–20):

> I have been crucified with Christ [the small and false self must die]. . . . and I live now not with my own life [it feels utterly inadequate and now unnecessary], but with the life of Christ who lives in me [realization of an indwelling, gratuitous Lover].

The Eastern Tradition referred to this process with the daring word *divinization*. We still feel presumptuous in claiming such an impossible inheritance. We like to earn things, but an inheritance can only be humbly received.

This classic pattern of transformation into *who we are in God* is called the paschal mystery. It is the only theme of each and every Eucharist—because it is so necessary to believe, and because we will do anything to avoid it. The liturgy slowly convinces us of who we are, although I have often said at Mass that it is easier for God to convince bread than it is to convince us! Bread knows, wine understands. Humans fight, deny, resist, and disbelieve anything for which they feel unready or unworthy. Thus, Jesus had to present the gift in the image of a resented banquet in

Luke 14:12–24. Paul speaks in the language of a free inheritance for those who would prefer to be slaves (Romans 8:14–17). In all cases, it feels like a wounding to our sophisticated soul. For some strange reason, love wounds us and beauty hurts us.

When the wound happens in a secular society like ours, we usually look for an immediate way to resolve it: playing the victim, mobilizing for vengeance (while sometimes calling it "justice"), or looking for someone to blame or to sue. A sacred culture would never bother with such charades and missed opportunities. Rather than a sacred wound, suffering for us often becomes a mere wound and, eventually, an embittering wound. The journey stops at that point and there's no future. Without the dignifying wound, there is no mystery, no greatness, no soul, and surely no Spirit. The theme is so constant in poetry, literature, and drama, that I wonder how we could continue to miss it: The wounded one is always the one with the gift; the comfortable one knows nothing.

What we have now in the West, by and large, is embittering wounds. The spiritual "machine" for turning wounds into glory has been lost by a secular people. Yet all the great mythologies and mystics tell us that we *will* be wounded, we *must* be wounded. It is what we do with the wounding that makes all the difference. There is something that we know after having passed through "the night sea journey" (an archetypal theme denoting a necessary trial of the would-be hero) that apparently we can know in no other way.

In classic tragedies, everyone sins and fails, but, somehow, they retain their human dignity. In classic comedy, everything is fine and dandy, but they all end up looking ridiculous. Life is a divine tragedy much more than a divine comedy, if I can dare to disagree with Dante.

Faith allows us to trust that God is in the suffering and the trials: "I thank you, Jesus, for what you want to teach me in this." Now understand, you won't say that on the first day, and probably not even on the second, but maybe on "the third day"! Such faithful people are literally indestructible, or, in Christian language, resurrected from the dead. This is one meaning of being "born again" and has more to do with having come through suffering alive and more whole than with an emotional experience after an altar call.

Ancient religions called it the inexorable wheel or the wheel of fortune, the mystery of life and death that just keeps turning. We have to take our time on the down side of the wheel and on the up side of the wheel—and learn in both parts of the cycle. That's why Jesus said the rich could not know what he was talking about (Mark 10:23–27), because they refuse to take their turn on the down side of the wheel. They try to buy their way out of absurdity, to avoid the essentially tragic nature of human existence by manufacturing a false path of comfort and control. Nothing new happens here. Nothing is transformed. The Holy One is not trusted. The self remains small.

Dying is not extraneous to life; it is a part of the mystery, and we do not understand life until we stand under death. Yet both sides of the mystery must be experienced and trusted. The Eastern religions speak of the *yin* and *yang* of things, nature religions simply speak of darkness and light, the Jewish people speak of slavery and deliverance, we Christians speak of death and resurrection. We are all pointing to God's universal pattern of trust and transformation. This is rightly spoken of as being "reborn," but has less to do with an emotional church experience than *a realigning life experience*.

Yes, God is dying in all things, but God is risen in all things too—and both at the same time! There is suffering in all things, as the Buddhists so honestly say. There's ecstasy in all things, as the Sufis so honestly say. There are both wild beasts and angels in the wilderness of human life, as the Gospels say (Mark 1:13). People who see "the better angels of our nature,"[24] while not avoiding the essentially tragic nature of human existence,[25] are always the seers, the mystics, the prophets, the great souls—the fuel that keeps history advancing.

Part of the great mystery of life is that it's just as hard to see the ecstasy and beauty of things as it is to accept the crucifixion of things. Both are the paschal mystery—Christ has died, Christ is risen—and both are an utter act of faith and surrender. In fact, when I see how the negative response comes first to most people, I wonder if the seeing of the Resurrection is not actually the harder act of faith. We find this in all four Gospel accounts, and I think it is more significant than we imagined—not just doubting Jesus's personal resurrection, but equally doubting our own, that of others, and the ability of God to turn all human crucifixions into a cosmic resurrection.

Romano Guardini (1885–1968) said something that I still don't like. I wish he had not said it, but I know it to be true. He said, "The imperfections of the Church are the Cross of Christ."[26] It was the high priests, the elders, and the scribes who turned Christ over for crucifixion. On the smaller level, it is also our closest friends and partners who often try us the most. Note the necessary betrayals of Peter and Judas. Betrayal *had* to happen (see John 17:12 and Acts 1:16). I don't fully understand why it is that way, but it seems that the very vehicles that proclaim and promote the Christ mystery in us are also its greatest obstacles!

Yet, this is also a consolation, because the broader church is only a larger reflection of me. The individual and the corporate Body seem to mirror one another, challenge one another, convert one another. The individual and the corporate Body are *foils* to one another. (A foil is any person or thing which, by strong contrast, underscores or enhances the other.) They are necessary foils, I suspect, although it often seems to work in only one direction. The individual believer must also be allowed to challenge the corporate Body to a deeper faithfulness to Jesus.

We shouldn't be too surprised at the common antagonisms within the church. We always hate truth when it's too close to us. We are always most capable of hating the people who are closest to us. We all know that the greatest antipathies are often between husband and wife, parent and child, Christian and other Christian. The mirror revealing our own shadow is held too close to our face. The church's closeness to Christ carries with it that same peril. It carries the weight of this great Christ mystery, and it knows what Christ will demand of the soul.

So, even though the church proclaims the Christ, it is, in fact, afraid of Christ. How could it not be? If we faced up to what Christ is actually saying, we would have to live up to it. So the Christian ego, struggling to survive, blocks and guards against the great Christ as he comes charging down the field of history. Strange, isn't it? But merely look at our record on slavery, the liberation of human sexuality, authoritarianism, racism, sexism, ecology, the rights of labor, materialism, militarism, nonviolence, and simplicity. These have not been areas of our strength, yet they follow from the direct teaching of Jesus. We divide over our designated leader, precisely because he *does* have authority in our life, just as children fight and resent their parents. Most of these issues were first recognized as issues by nonbelievers and then gradually validated as issues by Christian teaching.

Yet, we can neither doubt nor deny that the church still keeps promoting the mystery of Christ, almost in spite of itself. It raises up the sign and symbol so all of us can be seduced and drawn into the crucible of transformation. We fall in love with Jesus and his great gospel, and then spend the rest of our lives being opposed by the very one who gave us the gospel in the first place. Yet it is usually the great Tradition that gave us the very categories of truth, love, and justice that we throw back at that Tradition! People fight Christianity with Christian criteria! People resent the church with church categories! So God is winning anyway, and does not seem to care who gets the credit.

It seems unlikely at first, but when I see husbands and wives fighting one another, then I understand. We fight the one we love. We fight the love who's closest, who demands everything of us. We fight the love that demands we love it back. So it doesn't surprise me anymore, although it terribly disappoints me, that the church itself fights and blocks the gospel so much. I had once assumed that the "head office" would naturally be my backup, encouragement, and support. Many times it has been, as long as the stretch is not too far, so I am still grateful for this Church, which both mothers me and maddens me. My human mother did the same.

Connecting to the Real World

Today, I believe we have failed to produce real spirituality (or real holiness, if you prefer that word) in many adherents of religion. It is not readily apparent that a large percentage of baptized Christians are in love with God or, much less, "molded to the pattern of his death" (Philippians 3:10). We've "churched" many people, both good, sincere people and people who simply *like* religious trappings and language. But real transformation into a "new creation" is seldom the agenda. People living "through him, with him, and in him" (see Romans 11:36) are much less common than people pursuing a certain kind of positive self-image. The record of religion worldwide is not very good in promoting forgiveness, tolerance, compassion, and generosity. I have often said that I would sooner deal with the real sins of people who are living in the-True-Self-in-God than the virtues of people who are still living in the false self, which is now "religious." The world can do without such virtue.

There are three common stances in religion: (1) the old self on the occasional new path, (2) the new self on the new path, and (3) the new self on the occasional old path. The first is by far the most common and the most disappointing. The second is the perfect saint who hardly ever exists. The third is the real arena of growth and salvation for almost all human lives that I have ever encountered. It is what the New Testament calls "the saints."

Today, in many cases, we have a lot of ideological hysteria and junk religion—on both the left and the right (New Age and Jesus Seminar fundamentalism among some liberals; papal idolatry and nonhistorical orthodoxy among some conservatives[27]).

It's similar to junk food because it only satisfies enough to gratify the momentary desire but does not really feed the intellect or heart. Junk religion is usually characterized by fear of the present and fear of the future (which is really fear of God). What we hear when people have really met God is that there is no fear of the present because it is always full, there is no fear of the future because God's in charge, and there is no fear of the past because it has been healed and forgiven. Then people do not use God to avoid reality or to fabricate a private, self-serving reality, but let God lead them into the fullness of Reality: not *away from* dilemmas and paradoxes, but right *onto* the horns of the human dilemma![28]

Whatever reconstruction we're going to do cannot be based on fear or on reaction—even reaction against junk religion. It has to be based on *a positive and fully human experience* of God as a loving Presence. When we encounter a religion that is preoccupied with security, fear, or maintaining a positive self-image; when religion is punitive and acts as if it can lead someone to God through threat and coercion, this is junk religion. True religion is ready to let God be in charge, and to let God lead us into a new future that we do not yet understand— and no longer even need to understand.

The greatest Catholic moral theologian of the twentieth century, Bernard Häring (1912–1998), believed that many of the patterns and practices of present institutional religion reveal a *behavioral atheism*. We only need to be "control freaks" when we don't believe that God is in charge or when we can't trust God to be in charge. Practical atheism is probably the most common way that we all live. I know I do, most days of my life.

So, what must we surrender? Anxiety would be the natural starting place. I admit that takes a lot of letting go—and it takes all our life to begin to get there. In fact, we cannot *get* there at all—we are led, seduced, and drawn by the endless subterfuges of God. God, like a thief, steals our addictions from us. We can go back and work for justice, peace, and truth, but it will be a new self doing it—and, we hope, in a new and creative, win/win way.

David Ray Griffin writes of "transformative traditionalism,"[29] as opposed to cheap traditionalism that often keeps us inside of our comfort zones under the rubric of loyalty and orthodoxy. The patterns of how humans enter into relationship and destroy relationship are always the same. Maybe we've progressed in terms of science, medicine, technology, and building nice homes, but there's no reason for us to believe that the soul is any wiser than it was in any previous century. The recurring patterns in transformative Tradition are always patterns of growth, change, and repentance—which actually increase anxiety—and not just patterns of repetition to take away our anxiety. Transformative traditionalism leads us right into our anxieties, so we have to meet God and change—or die. The old-fashioned words for that are heaven, purgatory, and hell.

The Vital Information Needed to Survive

I've recommended to a lot of people Bill McKibben's book, *The Age of Missing Information*.[30] McKibben records everything that appears on cable television over a period of twenty-four hours in the early 1990s. In alternating chapters in his book, he analyzes what this is teaching him about the nature of reality.

Then he spends twenty-four hours sitting alone on the top of a mountain in the New York Adirondacks. In the interweaving chapters, he teaches what he learned in that twenty-four-hour period. His conclusion is that the vital information that human beings need to survive spiritually is learned more in silence than on any possible television show. It feels like a secular call to contemplation.

He says that we're being taught, not just useless information on TV, but very real patterns which numb, destroy, and make it impossible to access the vital wisdom that we need. Television is actually counterproductive—not only in its content, but in its form. For example, the very style of MTV and most commercials teaches us to be satisfied with strobe-light snapshots of life, with no beginning, middle, or end; no continuity or purpose beyond the stimulating images themselves. In MTV-land, there was simply episodic meaning, and the flood of disconnected images on social media continues that trend. We are back into deconstruction and a discontinuous world.

It is not good for the soul to be subjected to thousands of images that hint at sexuality and violence, without consequences. There's no character development, no continuity in relationship, no real suffering in the shootings, no price or meaning to that sexual gesture. All of this forms a foundational lie about the nature of reality, which is probably a simple definition of evil. We are not being well-served by mere stimulation. All the great religions actually taught methods of *under-stimulation* as the primary spiritual discipline.

Some might think this is overstated, but now I know why some people have gone so far as to take the television out of the house. They're desperate to rediscover meaning. They're desirous of reconstructing the world on some old, and also new, levels. For the most part, I see conservatives avoiding transformation and I see progressives avoiding traditions. All of us lose *the vital wisdom that is necessary for the soul to survive.*

Eucharist and Family Meal as Reconstructive Ritual

No group of people has any influence on history unless it has common rituals that name and demarcate the seasons and the meanings of their lives, both individually and collectively.

There certainly has been no more central symbol for Catholic Christianity than the celebration of the Eucharist. *Eucharistein* is the Greek word for giving thanks. Thus, the Eucharist is a thanksgiving meal. The early Christians combined the weekly Jewish scripture service and the Jewish Passover meal into one meal, intended as a symbol of universal table fellowship. In light of that, it is disappointing whenever it has become a symbol of ethnicity, worthiness, or group membership and loyalty.

Jesus's most common image for what he was doing in his three years of public ministry is the image of a wedding banquet. When he talked about the banquet, about the feast, there was always an endless table that had room for the outcasts, room for those who were not inside, who were somehow considered the outsiders. (See, for example, all the rule-breaking meals in Luke's Gospel, particularly Luke 14:1–24, or Matthew 22:9–10: "Go to the crossroads and invite everyone you can find to the wedding"—good and bad alike!)

In my experience of priesthood, Mass has been most effective and most exciting when the celebration is most clear and prayerful. When we can get down to the bare symbols, they're primal, compelling, and universal. As Mahatma Gandhi (1869–1948) said, "There are people in the world so hungry that God cannot appear to them except in the form of bread."[31] We so long for joy that God even risked coming into the world in the form of intoxication, through that perilous thing called wine. While its excess has caused so much suffering, for most of us wine nonetheless offers conviviality, communion, freedom, and even joy. The Eucharist, the sharing of the bread and wine, is a meal of communion. As if that were not enough, all the necessary symbols of transformation, according to C. G. Jung (1875–1961), are contained within the Catholic Mass.[32]

During these times of cultural transition, I see the priesthood being diminished and even disappearing in many places. What is God's message to our church in all of this? (I can only assume that God is doing this.) Maybe, at this time, we are being led back to our original Jewish roots. In Judaism, most of the major rituals, most of the major feast days, are not celebrated in the synagogue or the Temple, but around the family table. The mother and the father are clearly the priests of the meal. The sacred is located in the domestic, everyday world.

In a certain sense, some of our current confusion about the priesthood seems misplaced or even unnecessary. One way or another, the great celebration of the Eucharist, where families from various households gather together, will be maintained, perhaps on the great feast days and in local churches. Maybe priests need to be more like overseeing bishops, and the heads of families need to be more like priests! This will never please those with primary managerial concerns, but it will very much please those with concern for depth, family, and the power of the personal. "Location, location, location," the motto of successful entrepreneurs, makes a lot of sense spiritually too.

We must relocate religion in the universal and ubiquitous home, or we will continue to have a church of highly passive and even infantile levels of commitment. We priests must be humble enough to see that, with the best of intentions, we have castrated the historical spiritual leadership of the male, the father, the parents themselves. We moved religion to a level of organization where it was largely anonymous, impersonal, unaccountable, and therefore ineffective for most people. No wonder the store-front and Evangelical churches keep growing, while we retain an overwhelming number of members who want nothing more than to fulfill their weekly obligation.

We need to nurture the roles of spiritual mothers and spiritual fathers in our homes. God is present at our everyday tables, after all. Home meals ought to be faith-filled meals. Maybe God is telling us something in our current shortage of priests.

I don't think we need a lot of "middle management" when we have true spirituality. The product and the customer have to be kept close, immediate, and personally owned. The whole structure has to move down one full level, in my opinion. We need to rediscover the sanctity of the natural family as the basic institution of society. When we rediscover the sacred *there*, our fathers will know the priesthood of their fatherhood and our mothers will know the priesthood of their motherhood.

I use the word *priesthood* intentionally, because priesthood simply means the one who names the connection between the transcendent world and this world. If you make that connection, you're a priest. This is the priesthood that all Christians are called to by virtue of being baptized as "priest, prophet, and king" or "priestess, prophetess, and queen." Far too often, we institutional priests connect people with church more than with a daily spiritual life. It is the common substitution of the vehicle for the journey itself, the menu for the meal itself. As my friend Paula D'Arcy said so well when we taught together, "God comes disguised as your life."

We must be honest and say that the role of spiritual leadership has been abdicated by many Christian and Catholic mothers and fathers, handed over to the hierarchical priesthood and to ordained ministers. In fact, we Catholics have narrowed our understanding of priesthood so much that we only see priesthood in our ordained priests. "Holy Orders" are good and essential, but they must be balanced by some "Holy Non-Orders." It is not as if our success has been so overwhelming that we cannot imagine doing it better.

Yes, there will always be a place for classic, cathedral feast-day liturgy, but I would almost see it moving in two directions: the great magnificent feast and the daily or weekly family feast around the family table.

Recovering the sacred character of the family meal is a reconstructive act that is close at hand. I'm not talking about whipping through the classic family mealtime grace, "Bless us, O Lord, and these thy gifts, which we are about to receive from thy bounty through Christ our Lord, Amen." (I knew a family that used to practice how fast they could say it just to shock guests!) I'm talking about more than the simple grace at meals: perhaps a reading now and then, perhaps a guided conversation on a specific topic—almost anything, where the father and mother take on their role as mentors, guides, spiritual leaders of the whole.

Rituals create families, in a sense. Any parent knows that when they do something at least two years in a row, the little ones wait for it in the third year. Children have a natural sense of timing, ritual, seasons, and feasts. Ritual is the key to re-sacralizing the home. I don't want to suggest the particular rituals that a family should name and claim. Certainly, each family has its own customs, and there are a number of religious resources that suggest new family rituals for those who need ideas. I'm saying that we need to take this more seriously, especially during the current cultural crisis. It could well be enough to hold our culture and society together, because it starts with the basic social building block of meaning—the natural family. We jumped it up a level to the spiritual family before the smaller unit was evangelized.

We must rediscover the Eucharist—and, indeed, our own family meals—as feasts of God's magnanimity, as celebrations of God's gracious givenness to this work-a-day world. We must trust that the material world can be an adequate sign of the spiritual world, in things as ordinary as bread and wine, as common as the family meal. We must see their sacramental nature. Priestly sacraments are overdone when they lose a true sacramental understanding of reality. We do not have to leave the ordinary world to find the holy. We clergy are doing God no favor by keeping "the holy" under our jurisdiction.

There were two places where I have found Catholic prayer life to be located in the home, around family altars and family prayer: the Philippine Islands and Kerala in South India. In both places, I met some of the most fervent and in-depth Catholics in the world. The head of the Capuchin Mission Office wrote some years ago that he could make a statistical case that those places where Mass has been offered most scrupulously are the very countries where the faith is most weak and passive.[33] That is scary, even if it is only half true. We can do better, and I am convinced that we will. History is forcing us. God is therefore inviting us.

Four

Transformation

We would think that the unexpected brings the most stress to our lives, but psychologists say that planned change is even more disruptive than unplanned change. Somehow, things that "just happen" are seen as acts of God. We can fight them, ignore them, or accept them, but we know we can't fix them or change them. So, after the initial shock or disappointment, we find the energy to deal with them. We find the grace to rise to the occasion. But when we think there's some malicious or lesser mind at work, or that we could have changed something by wile or guile, we fight it, fret over it, and never stop fussing, at least internally. That's stress.

For the past fifty years, we've been experts at *planning* change. That is a new phenomenon for the most part. Unfortunately, it has now become a mindset and a way of life. We think we can do it and that we *ought* to be doing it. That's not to say that some of the changes we've brought about, in church and society, weren't good and necessary, but I think we have paid a large price internally for such a Promethean, daringly original self-image. For the most part, we can no longer just "let it be." We are now natural fixers, changers, adjustors—constant engineers of our own reality. It makes for a very different kind of soul. It develops what I call the calculative mind, as opposed to the goal of all mature spirituality: the contemplative mind.

The attitude that is needed for deep and panoramic seeing is not a fixing, calculating stance, but much more an attitude of listening, trusting, and waiting. It is the only way "to get out of the way" with our judgments, control mechanisms, and personal opinions. Maybe that's why Jesus says we are saved by faith, by trusting and surrendering instead of pushing and trying, and by passion (the *suffering of* reality) rather than deliberate action. Interestingly, we say we are saved by the passion, death, and resurrection of Jesus—all things that are done *to* him more than anything he does.

It seems that the human person needs an Absolute outside of itself. Have you noticed how much the enthusiastic types on television or radio use the word *absolutely*—even when they're talking about an exercise machine?! In an age when we have no real absolutes, the whirling mind and emotions look for something upon which to settle in order to take away their anxiety. We seem to need an outer reference point to stop the vertigo of our own imagination and the tyranny of having to make constant choices. We seem to need some kind of god to serve as a centerpiece. "I will create an absolute for myself to justify and settle my choices: my football team, my marriage, my religion, my land, my theory, my self-image, my rights, my exercise machine—anything at all. Just give me something to wrap my thoughts and feelings around for a while, something outside of myself—an idea, an event, a person, a project—to free me from the boredom and tyranny of myself!" *It works* and gives us a settled sense of purpose and direction. Without it, we find it very hard to live with our own mind and emotions.

The idea is not wrong, just misplaced. The only real issue is to find an absolute that really has *some* Absolute character to it. That is probably the difference between a wise person and a merely opinionated person. Wisdom knows what is worth worshiping and honoring; the rest of us will settle for anything to get us through the next conversation. I believe that everybody has faith in something in order to survive, even if it is faith in cynicism. We all find something upon which to lean, and false gods do work for short periods. We all find some absolute around which to whirl, even if it is an absolute opinion that there is no God.

I use the concepts of faith and the contemplative mind almost interchangeably. For me, they are the same reality, both describing the trustful and God-centered way that we can allow ourselves to be used. In this *different mind*, we do not so much try to change reality or others, as allow ourselves to be changed, so that we can be *useable for God*. It is not so important *what* we do now—as *the who that is doing it*. This is crucial and is at the heart of what we mean by that amorphous word *holiness*. There is a radically transformed experience of the *I* when we are "holy," both within ourselves and noticed by those who observe us. The private "I" has been transformed into a Larger Self that believers would call God. "I live no longer not I . . ." (see Galatians 2:20).

The Belly of the Whale

The word *change* normally refers to new beginnings. But transformation, the mystery we're examining, more often *happens not when something new begins, but when something old falls apart*. The pain of something old falling apart—chaos—invites the soul to listen at a deeper level. It invites, and sometimes forces, the soul to go to a new place because the old place is falling apart. Most of us would never go to new places in any other way. The mystics use many words to describe this chaos: fire, dark night, death, emptiness, abandonment, trial, the Evil One. Whatever it is, it does not feel good and it does not feel like God. We will do *anything* to keep the old thing from falling apart. This is when we need patience and guidance, and the *freedom to let go* instead of tightening our controls and certitudes. Perhaps Jesus is describing just this phenomenon when he says, "It is a narrow gate and a hard road that leads to life, and only a few find it" (Matthew 7:13–14). Not accidentally, he mentions this narrow road right after teaching the Golden Rule. He knows how much letting go it takes to "treat others as you would like them to treat you" (7:12).

So, a change can force a transformation. Spiritual transformation always includes a usually disconcerting reorientation. It can either help people to find a new meaning or it can force people to close down and slowly turn bitter. The difference is determined precisely by the quality of our inner life, our spirituality. Change happens, but transformation is always a process of letting go, living in the confusing, shadowy space for a while, and eventually being spit up on a new and unexpected shore. You can see why Jonah in the belly of the whale is such an important symbol for many Jews and Christians.

In moments of insecurity and crisis, shoulds and oughts don't really help; they just *increase* the shame, guilt, pressure, and likelihood of backsliding. It's the deep *yes*es that carry us through. It's that deeper something we are strongly *for* that allows us to wait it out. It's someone in whom we absolutely believe and to whom we commit. In plain language, love wins out over guilt any day. It is sad that we settle for the short-run effectiveness of shaming people instead of the long-term life benefits of true transformation. But then, we are a culture of product and efficiency, not terribly patient with growth. God clearly is much more patient—and, finally, much more effective. God lets Jonah run in the wrong direction, but finds a long, suffering, circuitous path to get him back where he needs to be—in spite of himself! That is patiently supporting inner transformation. Only God seems to have developed such a talent. We usually prefer order, control, predictability, and immediacy. I think that is probably the most striking difference between institutional religion and the God of mercy.

The Loss of Criteria

The previous personal, theistic worldview saw things in terms of what was often called the Great Chain of Being. The great monotheistic religions held God as a clear outer reference point that grounded and originated all things. All lower things were understood in terms of the higher, which gave them an essential importance in the universe. Everything belonged and mirrored the Highest. Within the Great Chain of Being (which I will explore in more detail in Chapter Eight), everything was *intrinsically* connected and had *inherent* dignity and meaning. The order was typically (1) the Divine Realm, (2) the realm of heaven and angels, (3) the human, (4) the animal, (5) the vegetable, (6) the waters and minerals in the earth, and (7) the earth itself, which held them all together.

These were all linked in purpose, meaning, and sacredness. Some contemporary metaphors for the same are the seamless garment, a cosmic egg (to be examined in Chapter Five), spiritual ecology, and the integrity of all creation. As long as there is a Transcendent reference point, an outer Sacred Source which communicates Itself, then there is inherent and pervasive meaning in all the other links in the chain. It's an enchanted and coherent universe, inside of which almost all peoples have lived since the beginning of human history. Nothing is profane once we have learned how to see. We are the sad exceptions, living in a dualistic and finally shattered universe, which is no longer a *uni-verse* ("that which turns around one") at all.

Almost all peoples who have lived on the planet were absolutely certain about the Highest and therefore moved downward and outward with clarity and noble assurance. This certainty created an objective criterion and reference point for naming the good, the true, and the beautiful. Thus, Saint Francis could even see the divine image in a worm! If there is a creator, then everything else is a creature and, in part, reflects the divine image.

Either we see God in everything or we have lost the basis for seeing God in anything. Once the dualistic mind takes over, the ego is in a "pick, choose, and decide" game, which is the beginning of exclusionary, punishing, and even violent religion. Remember, anthropologically, religion begins with the making of a distinction between the pure and the impure. Jesus consistently ignores such a distinction. In fact, it is at the heart of almost half of his gospel actions!

For postmodernism, on the other hand, everything is relative. (That, of course, is ultimately indefensible, because if everything is relative then that principle is relative too.) Because the contemporary mind has decided that everything is relative instead of relational (a theistic or personalized universe), it forces the individual to manufacture ("make by hand") his or her own greatness. Perhaps we have confused relative with relational. Relative thinking allows us to dismiss or decrease the energy in everything; relational thinking allows us to increase the energy and kneel in awe before God-in-all-things. I call the first depreciators and the second appreciators.

If God is not the center, *we* are burdened with being the center. What an impossible and self-defeating task. Moment by moment, I am at the whim of whimsical desire. "What do *I* want?" or "Am I important now?" become wrong first questions and keep us trapped in pettiness. Secular people are burdened with finding their own meaning and their private significance— by themselves! It's an impossible and self-defeating task.

Without the inherent dignity that comes from who-we-are-in-God, we have to become more and more outrageous, more and more bizarre, more and more exaggerated or isolated to make sure that we stand out amid billions of people. The eccentric is the one who lives *outside the center*. We expect this of a young person, who is still finding his or her Center, but now many in their eighties still live with such fragile or over-padded egos. We are no longer living in a wisdom culture when even age does not lead to foundation and ground.

Postmodernism ends up with what some call *reductionism*. We can no longer start from the top and find universal meaning reflected through all of creation. Everything is disconnected, standing on its own, unable to validate itself apart from itself. Everything is diminished and demystified. So, the best we can normally do is take the lowest level that we can control and understand and move up from there—if we can move up at all. The language of the reductionist often begins with "only" or "just," with suspicion and cynicism. This language will determine ahead of time how much we can see. (Ken Wilber, although not a Christian, sees this pattern as the anemic and incomplete viewpoint of our time. Read almost anything by him if you want to be mightily challenged and moved beyond the reductionist postmodern mind.)

The reductionist and suspicious mind is trapped in a world where it can always be "in charge," which is only at the smallest level and with the most insecure self—our own tiny moment of history, our limited individual capacity to understand. Nothing great comes from reductionism or suspicious minds, except to initially clear away the bogus issues. Faith, instead, is the exact opposite. *Faith, in its most universal sense, is openness to magnanimity, mystery, and more.* We do not have to be "religious" to know that is true.

Richard Tarnas helped me to recognize how each century is trapped in its own web, its own limited categories, its own limited way of understanding. Presently, for example, we are trapped in a "market" worldview. This worldview is very pragmatic and individualistic and uses the language of romantic expressionism: "I have" and "I choose" are the power statements. Our worldview does not care about greater histories, greater philosophies, greater thinkers, or about anything much except the market world of buying and selling. All of us, even Christians, usually find ourselves trapped inside of exchange values instead of inherent values.

We must be careful that each new revolutionary insight does not return us to our suspicious and deconstructive preferences. I do not disagree, for example, with the feminist critique that we have not heard from women very much in history (or minorities, or gays, or the poor, or the losers of any category, for that matter), but are we really going to say that Aristotle and Erasmus were not gifts to humanity because they happened to be male, or that Johanna Doe has the truth now because she is a woman? These understandable but knee-jerk reactions to new insights make new ideas more deconstructive than constructive. They only put in place another ten-year period of over-defensiveness and over-compensation. We don't have time for that anymore.

Such either/or deconstructionism has unfortunately given academia a very bad name—especially in a country like the United States, which needs all the educated, good minds it can get because of its immense worldwide influence. In a certain sense, we had a deconstructionist attitude from the beginnings of the American Revolution, never trusting higher class or culture, or that there might be a good meaning to "nobility." Yet, it was noble-minded men and women who fortunately led us beyond an anti-England or anti-anything perspective to a positive and visionary American Project. In general, deconstructionist attitudes are only helpful for initial clarity and focus. Of themselves, they provide no positive or creative foundation upon which to build for the long term.

Gospel Leaven

Postmodernism has tried to overcome the emptiness, or nihilism, of modernism by refusing to commit itself to any worldview. It could be called a moveable famine and has no comparable precedent in all of human history. Admittedly, modernism's technological, scientific explanation of everything did not feed the soul; it was, and is, empty of deep meaning. So, rather than not be fed, we moved one step further into famine by refusing to be committed to any sustaining food. *Skepticism* is another way to avoid ever having to place our bet, and therefore ever getting hurt. Universal skepticism is a common thought process today; critical thinking often looks like intelligence, and sometimes is. A bishop could be totally suspicious and skeptical, yet never be called a heretic! Strange, isn't it?

Skepticism and criticism are fail-safe protection measures for the psyche, but when they dominate, something deeper and more important has been abdicated. The human qualities of deference, patience, humility, risk-taking, and social grace are also needed for culture and its continuance. Humans grow in such a garden. Jesus does not encourage or expect a world where people are never hurt, or never suffer guilt or injustice. His entire concern is *what we do with mistakes when they happen— always knowing that they will*. Forgiving "seventy times seven" (Matthew 18:22) is a medicine for a healing community, not for a community with all the answers beforehand and all the appropriate punishments afterward.

After you've loved and failed a few times, you become afraid to love again. After you have suffered, as the world has suffered through the hundred million humans killed in war in the twentieth century, you are sure to create ways to protect yourself so that you will not have to suffer again. Postmodernism is a way out: no commitments, no surrenders, no absolute anything, no passion for anything—and, therefore, no disappointment, no hurt. On a certain level it makes sense, but, through the lessons of the Crucified, we are learning a different way. We can't avoid persecution. In fact, our assumption is that Jesus's lifestyle will probably lead to some new forms of persecution.

When we give ourselves to the mystery of Christ, we give ourselves to being hurt, to being on the wheel of life, to walking what we call the Way of the Cross. No wonder so much of the world resists it! Who wants to be on that wheel? Who wants to enter into solidarity with the tragic mystery of things? Who wants to be formed by the left hand of God? Who wants to bear the suffering? Few, I would think; only those who have been led through the mystery of death and resurrection and come out larger and awake. (That's probably what the Tradition means by those oft-misunderstood words *chosenness* or *election*.) In that sense, I say Christianity was intended by Jesus to be a minority position and always will be. He wasn't dividing the world into those God loved and those God didn't love. *Jesus was creating a remnant who were useable by God—to keep the whole world from its violent path toward self-destruction. Jesus was loving and drawing all of us into God,* or, as John put it, "to gather together into one the scattered children of God" (John 11:52). That is very different than forming a new tribe of saved and superior people.

All I see Jesus talking about is being light, being yeast, being salt, and being mustard seed. This is rather prominent, both at the beginning of his inaugural address (Matthew 5:13–16) and in his parabolic discourse (Luke 13:18–21). It's hard to believe that we missed it in favor of visions of Christendom, "moral majorities," managerial institutions, electorates, and "your excellencies." It kept us in the imperial ego-mind, as opposed to the surrendered, trusting mind of Jesus. It seems that, in earthly terms, all Jesus ever intended was a yeast of truth that would be a change agent or leavener in history. Ironically, Jesus and his disciples looked much more like an immoral minority than any moral majority! His plan was truly subversive and is the only one that ever has a chance of true victory. As Ambrose Bierce (1842–1914) said, a Conservative is "a statesman who is enamored of existing evils, as distinguished from the Liberal, who wishes to replace them with others."[34]

The gospel is beyond this whole mindset. The story line haunts us all, and still disappoints pretenders to power on left or right. The Jesus story stands as a revelatory judgment on every other story line, trial, and legal system in the world. It is still a shock and even a disappointment: *Jesus has a lot of hope in sinners* (which is good news for just about everybody). *Jesus only has problems with those who don't think they are sinners*. This turns all religious history upside down. The search for so-called purity is over. Now the only issue is honesty and humility. We call it by the hard word *repentance*.

In any human scenario, even when we don't want to believe it, we know that there are at least and always three characters: Jesus, the bad guys, and the supposed good guys. What Jesus says is, be prepared to be surprised about who is who. This leaven of the gospel is inexorably chipping away at such things as capital punishment, wars against the poor, war rationales in general, legal systems, idealizations of the wealthy and those at the top, and traditions of human torture and oppression.

The gospel story line will have the final chapter of history. God is winning, and that is good news for *all* the people, especially for those who don't yet know they are also "under the mercy."[35] Again and again, it creates an ability for humanity to "pull down the mighty from their thrones and lift up the lowly" (Luke 1:52). It is no accident that these revolutionary words come from Mary, the feminine first believer in Jesus.

Man-Movement-Machine-Monument-Memory

It seems that all great things in history start with an individual person. For the sake of alliteration and memory I will say *man*. If that person has something to say that is alive and real, and names reality well, it often moves to the second stage of becoming a *movement*. That's the period of the greatest energy. The church, for example, is at its greatest vitality as "the God Movement," and the institution is merely the vehicle for that movement. Neither pope nor president can ever control the movement itself, through any theology, doctrine, or dogma. We cannot control the blowing of the Spirit. It is to the mature credit of the Roman Catholic Church that it was able to teach this officially at the time of the Second Vatican Council.[36] The movement stage is always very exciting, creative—and also risky.

It's risky because the movement of God in history is larger than any denomination, any culture, or any tradition's ability to verbalize it. We feel out of control here, and yet why would anybody want it to be anything less than that? Do we really want to think that the great God could be in our little pockets? Would we respect a God that we could control? Would we really respect a church that presumed it could predict and contain God's actions? I don't think so, yet that is what so much immature religion seems to want—control over God by worshiping God "correctly." Thus, we move rather quickly out and beyond the dangerous movement stage to the machine stage. This is predictable and understandable, even if also unfortunate.

The institutional or *machine* stage of a movement will necessarily be *a less-alive manifestation*, which is not bad, although always surprising for those who see church as an end in itself instead of merely a vehicle for the vision. We need "the less noble" parts of the Body to keep us all growing toward love (1 Corinthians 12:22–24). We can also learn from the less-mature stages of life. The steps to maturity, in fact, are always steps through immaturity. There is no other way, but when we do not realize the limited capacities of a machine, we try to make it into something more than it is. We make it a *monument*, a closed system operating inside of its own, often self-serving, logic.

It's the nature of the beast and a seemingly inevitable movement, especially as we get tied up with job security, consistent policies for everything, and public image and identity. As soon as we get employment norms and professional people whose jobs depend on status, security, and dependability, it's very hard to take risks for God or for gospel values. Eventually this monument, and its maintenance and self-preservation, become ends in themselves. Jeremiah rails against such formalization at the beginning of his prophecy: "Put no trust in delusive words like, 'the temple, the temple, the temple!' While you follow alien gods . . . I am not blind—it is Yahweh who speaks" (see 7:4–11).

Monuments need to be regularly deconstructed and rebuilt. Thus Thomas Jefferson (1743–1826) believed that revolution had to be repeated in some form every twenty years![37]

Truth is never actualized until it becomes *my* truth—suffered, owned, and internalized. Surely authentic religion can settle for nothing less. Let me use here a clarifying and dense quote from John Stuart Mill (1806–1873). He is warning us against the monument and machine stages:

> Even if the received opinion be not only true, but the whole truth; unless it is suffered to be, and actually is, vigorously and earnestly contested, it will, by most of those who receive it, *be held in the manner of a prejudice*, with little comprehension or feeling of its rational grounds.[38]

Each generation has to appropriate its deepest beliefs for itself. We used to say it this way: "God has no grandchildren." Each generation must itself be realigned with God and discover the mystery for itself. Yet we want the results of someone else's homework. A machine-become-monument is now in place. It is so easy to just step on board, without ever knowing why or feeling the longing ourselves. We have entirely jumped over the man and movement stages and have "God's frozen people" instead of any hint of chosen, beloved, or journey status. In this state, religion is merely an excuse to remain unconscious, a *memory* of something that must once have been a great adventure. Now religion is no longer life itself, but actually a substitute for life or, worse, an avoidance of life. But God has no grandchildren; only children. The secret is to know how to keep in touch with the man and movement stages, without being naïve about the necessity of some machine and the inevitability of those who love monuments. We must also be honest: All of us love monuments when they are monuments to *our* man, our movement, or our machine.

Ordinary People

Sometimes machine and monument folks can be recaptured by the vision of the man and the movement. At the Center for Action and Contemplation in Albuquerque, New Mexico, we were often visited by our friend Frank Strabala (who died in 1999). He worked for the nuclear test site outside of Las Vegas, Nevada. In fact, Frank headed the operation for a number of years—and then dared, by the grace of the gospel, to call it into question. He even joined me once as we practiced civil disobedience at the test site. I will never forget seeing him walking toward me with a half-worried half-smile on his face. "I have trusted your teaching all these years. Now I have to trust where it has led me," he said. We stood together as his former employees drove by and gave less-than-flattering gestures to their old boss. I was humbled and awed by such courage and such humility. He had let go of his secure monument through an encounter with the man Jesus and the vision of the peace movement.

It's hard, and very rare, to call your own job into question. When Jesus called his disciples, he also called them away from their jobs and their families (see, for example, Matthew 4:22). Now, jobs and families don't sound like bad things, do they? He called them to leave their nets because as long as anyone is tied to job security, there are a lot of things they cannot see and cannot say. This is one of the great recurring disadvantages of clergy earning their salary from the church, and perhaps why Saint Francis did not want us to be ordained priests. We tend to think and say whatever won't undermine the company store.

Anyone who has ever worked for another person understands this, and I wonder if it is not at the root of so much anti-clericalism among the blue-collar workers of the world. They often see right through our clergy pretensions. As one smart construction worker once angrily said to me, "Would you really bother to try to prove or defend papal infallibility or who can 'transubstantiate' if you did not have a vested interest in the answer? Those are the prefab answers of people in management, but they are not even the questions of those in labor!" Wow. We must be humble enough to hear. I know he has a point when I see the glazed eyes of parents in the front pew as we sermonize about the glories of Holy Orders and celibacy!

Jesus called the disciples away from their natural families too. If there's another blindness that keeps us from bigger truth—an even more sacred cow than job—it is family. Families are either very good or very bad for human growth but, in either case, they are only runways for takeoff. As others have said, family provides roots, but the wings have to come from elsewhere.

What if we each went home tonight, gathered the kids in a circle, and said, "We are getting rid of the TV"? That would be very hard to do without a larger support system. Those kinds of wings, to a larger world, seldom can be grown inside of the nuclear family. All we can do is give the foundation of love and security so that they can ask such daring questions later; those questions usually cannot come from home. In fact, family holds many people behind a very safe and often small "white picket fence." It is not even roots for many people, much less wings— only a restricting brick wall.

That's why Jesus insists on asking bigger questions than the immediate family usually can. Jesus tells us not to get too secure in our job or assume that our small family has all the answers. This seems to be an Eastern wisdom that is more common in Asiatic cultures. The small family is very tight, but also tightly ensconced inside of extended family, neighborhood, religion, and traditions. Sadly, we have neither!

In India, for example, the four stages of a full life are student, householder, forest dweller/seeker, and, finally, wise elder. People cannot get on to the third and last stages of life until they have left the second. In the practical West, we stop at stage two, and increasingly do not have the skills for living even that stage well. I am sure this is part of the explanation for why our wisdom is so small, as are our insular politics and our tribal view of so much of the church.

Most of our men have not made many journeys away from "Mama"—and maternal churches and companies.[39] Because men have not undergone their spiritual journey, many spend the rest of their lives trying to marry Mama (ask many wives), afraid of any real intimacy with women, or needing the security systems that Mama always provides.

As a priest of almost fifty years, I am continually struck by how many of our most fervent Catholic men (including priests) are also very soft and security-conscious men, not risk-takers in any sense. Mama Church and Mother Mary dressed in blue are preferred to the Sermon on the Mount or forty days in *any* desert. This has profoundly affected the very character of the gospel that has been preached. We have not yet left home, so the gospel itself is highly domesticated.

When the safe assumptions of society and family reach the monument stage, you might think you need TNT or major surgery to break through. But you never win with any frontal attack on the mystery of evil. If you attack something directly, you let it determine the energy, the style, the opposition. You soon become the same thing, but in a better-disguised and denied form. Jesus calls that trying to drive out the devil by the prince of devils (see Luke 11:14–22). That's how evil expands so successfully. The disguise is almost perfect and, without spiritual discernment, will fool the best of us.

So, instead, Francis of Assisi went out to the edge and did it better. Francis respected the monuments, even loved them, but also went back to the original dynamism and nonviolent style of Jesus the man for his inspiration.

Assisi is surrounded by city walls. Inside those walls are the cathedral and the established churches, all of which are fine. That's where Francis first heard the gospel and fell in love with Jesus. But, then, he quietly went outside the walls and re-built some old ruins called San Damiano and the Portiuncula. He wasn't, with his mouth, telling the others they were doing it wrong. He just gently, lovingly tried to do it better. I think that's true reconstruction. Remember, *the best criticism of the bad is the practice of the better.* That might be a perfect motto for all reconstructive work. It does not destroy machines or even monuments but reinvigorates them with new energy and form.

San Damiano was still a church building, but it was small, poor, and on the edge. Francis transformed it.

Moral Realism

There is a book called *The Ignorant Perfection of Ordinary People*.[40] The brilliant title says it all. In it, Robert Inchausti speaks of the spiritual longings of ordinary people as the basis for most great social and political reforms. He calls it, so rightly, Constructive Postmodernism! This is exactly what we are talking about here: People who know the challenges but build anyway. This is not naïve denial, not Pollyanna idealism, not utopianism, but the true biblical *hope that is received only on the other side of suffering and failure*. Most of us either become paralyzed or think we are enlightened because we know about the problems, the sin, the scandal, the essentially tragic nature of human existence. We go through the deconstructive stage without the reconstructive gift of vision and hope. That's probably the main burden of being a nonbeliever or a mere ideologue: the forlorn or cynical attitude of so many academics and social activists.

I meet people of "ignorant perfection" every now and then, and I am always in awe of God's subtle work of art in them. It is like meeting an unselfconscious but strikingly beautiful man or woman. These folks are usually traditional in their values. Maybe they still appear to be "first naïveté" people. They're usually very commonsensical. There's a moral realism in healthy and grounded people. They're not ideological, on the left or the right. They can accept people whom others have judged for one reason or another. They don't move up in their head and form great big explanations for why something is wrong or right. You can never shock them. They do not read reality, first of all, with their moral compass, but with the eyes of compassion. They don't bring answers down from above, but find them within and evoke them from below. Also, for some reason, they don't compare. They take what is right in front of them on its own, self-evident terms, giving each person the benefit of the doubt.

I think I love and look for people like this because my father, Richard Rohr (1910–1999), Kansas farmer and railroad worker, was that kind of man. I have also met simple nuns who work with prostitutes and orderlies at the jail, who deal patiently with whatever is right in front of them, not even thinking to call it patience. Somehow, they have been rebuilt in a new form. My assumption is that at one point they were "unbuilt," stripped down to the core, and learned how to live from that clear and humbled point.

This moral realism is not a moral skepticism or abdication, but, ironically, a true and enlightened traditionalism. Only the shape of human sin changes in each age; we are always pointing to the same illusions and false promises of the ego (thus, the perennial truth of ancient typologies like the Enneagram, and the capital sins or "demons" of most traditions). The patterns through which each generation must maneuver are the same as our ancestors, and someone who has once touched the face and name of sin in themselves is never shocked again. Evil, like God, is One, which is probably why we personified it in Satan. But, once we smell the scent of Satan, it shows up in all kinds of shapes and forms, none of which surprises us anymore. They only sharpen us.

What has made this sharpening difficult is that all the information (not wisdom) since the beginning of time has become exponentially available in the last generation. We are always expecting the final and truthful answer to show itself. This explosion of data makes us think that wisdom is still out in front of us. Unfortunately, we turn away from the pregnant "now," from our ancestors, and from the healing power of memory. We reject healthy traditionalism, even transformative traditionalism, in favor of a future answer that is never quite here—because, almost as soon as it arrives, it is rejected as an "old" idea when another guru appears on the scene. Just watch the flow of self-help books and how quickly their fleeting fame passes.

By very traditional wisdom or moral realism, I refer to qualities or states of being such as silence, solitude, detachment, honesty, confession, forgiveness, and radical humility. No new author or book is going to do better than these. We hope any new material will just help us understand them better. There is also nothing very spectacular about any of these disciplines— no dependence on crystals, prophecies, auspicious days, or a highly trained priestly class. Ordinary people discover this wisdom by *living*!

Probably the single most traditional wisdom issue is, of course, the immense teaching capacity of human suffering, and especially unjust suffering. Probably none of the world religions deals with it in a more up-front and utterly dramatic way than Christianity. We are, after all, the only religion that worships the victim. As discussed earlier in this book, we proclaimed the scapegoated one to represent all we deny and reject. It seems that God must be trying to address a very central human problem in coming among us as a crucified and forgiving Victim. I ask again, isn't this—sooner or later—at the heart of everybody's spiritual problem: what we do with our pain?

Why evil? Why suffering? Even Job can't get an answer, and Job, I think, is the epitome of moral development in the Hebrew Scriptures. His is the same story as Jesus. Job begs for the answer, and finally trusts when he knows that God is taking him seriously and he is simply *in the conversation* (see Job 42:1–6). Jesus later *becomes* the answer in his passion, death, and resurrection, but it is really the same answer: God can be trusted. The world is still safe, coherent, and even blessed. We are saved by being addressed and included in a cosmic conversation. We do not really need answers; we only need to be taken seriously as part of the dialogue. But we only know this in hindsight, after the suffering and the struggle. It cannot be known theoretically, theologically, or before the fact. That is the big rub, the perennial disappointment. I cannot copy from someone else's homework. I can only be inspired by it, which is a good start.

Our knowledge of God is participatory. God refuses to be intellectually "thought," and is only known in the passion and pain of it all, when the issues become soul-sized and worthy of us. Saint Catherine of Genoa (1447–1510), a laywoman and mystic, is supposed to have asked Jesus, in one of her locutions, why there is so much pain and suffering on the earth. Jesus responded that, if there was any other way, he would have thought of it.

There's no other way we learn how to let go and discover compassion, it seems. There is no other way that we will give up control until we are led to the limits of our own resources—and must rely upon another. Then we know the Ground of our Being. Don't trust any spiritual teacher who has not suffered—and don't look for any teacher who predicts the future, only one who can lead you to peace with the past and, especially, with the sufferings of the past.

Five

The Cosmic Egg of Meaning

If we are going to be the rebuilders of society, we need to be rebuilt ourselves. A healthy psyche lives within at least three containers of meaning. Imagine three domes, or levels, of meaning. The first is called My Story, the second is Our Story, and the third is *The* Story. This is what I call the cosmic egg. It is the unique and almost unconscious gift of all healthy religion. Much of the genius of the biblical revelation is that it honors and integrates all three. Much of the weakness of deconstructed society is that it usually honors only one level at best, and thus treats that level very poorly. Most postmodern people are trapped inside the smallest container if they are secular individualists, in the second container if they are merely cultural conservatives, and in a false version of the third if they are fundamentalist in any form. The saint/whole/healed person lives happily inside of all three.

I. This Is Me (My Story)

The modern, and now postmodern, world is the first period of history where a large number of people have been allowed to take their private lives and identities seriously. Many of our parents did not even have a language for it. There is a wonderful movement into individuation here, but there is also a diminishment and fragility if that is all we have. (*Individuation*,

THE COSMIC EGG

The **Story**
What is

Our **Story**
We are
Group identities and
loyalties that expand
our sense of self

My **Story**
Just me
Private, small life
searching for significance
through power, prestige
and possessions

The great patterns
that are always true

Ethnicity, groupthink

Nationalism,
cultural religion

Saves us from the illusion of "we"
and the smallness of "me"

*Healthy and biblical religion
includes the whole cosmic egg.*

by the way, is a positive word to describe an appropriate sense of self, ego, and boundaries. Individualism, however, refers to the *exaggerated* sense of self, ego, and overprotected boundaries.)

In this first dome is my private life: those issues that make me special, inferior or superior, right or wrong, handicapped or gifted, depending on how "I" see it. "I" and my feelings and opinions are the reference point for everything. We must let go of exactly this in early prayer practice, and yet this is the very tiny and false self that contemporary people take as normative, and even sufficient.

The dome of This Is Me is about all the postmodern person has left: my power, my prestige, and my possessions. It's the little stage where I do *my* dance and where the questions are usually, "Who is watching me? How do *I* feel? What do *I* believe? What makes me unique?" It's a passing arena, to be certain. It will be over in a few years and is frankly boring if it is all we have to talk about. My Story is not big enough or true enough to create large or meaningful patterns by itself.

But many people live their whole lives at this level of anecdote and nurtured self-image, without ever connecting with the larger domes of meaning. They *are* what they have done and what has been done to them—nothing more. You can see how fragile and unprotected, and therefore constantly striving, this self will be. It is very easily offended, fearful, and therefore often posturing and pretentious.

My opinion is that, if we stay in this smallest dome of meaning, we often move toward a neurotic self-image. Jean Houston put it this way: "When mythic material remains latent, unused and unexplored, it can lead to pathological behavior."[41] This small and fragile self needs to be a part of something more significant—and so it creates dramas, tragedies, and victimhoods to put itself on a larger stage. Just watch American television, where trivia and drivel are raised to an art form— as much by the news, political commentators, and religious programming as by the easily criticized talk shows. Unfortunately, that's the primary paradigm out of which we live today: merely episodic meaning, bolstering the tiny and disconnected self. A woman claims to be receiving apparitions from Mary. A gunman wants to get his picture in the news. Both are isolated and episodic, but trying to be cosmic.

I once saw a cartoon that depicted a pair of restroom doors. Instead of one door saying Men and one saying Women, the first said Evil Oppressors and the second said Victims. What a simplistic and, finally, destructive way to image reality, yet that is our recent politically correct framework. It gives the small self a sense of being a part of some national drama, as we constantly decide who is which—who is bad and who is the hero. Life as a giant whodunit seems to be the secular form of heaven and hell.

The small self is intrinsically unhappy because it has no ontological foundation. It is not real. It does not exist. It will always be insecure, afraid, and scrambling for significance. The purely secular project is doomed to creating catastrophe. The stage isn't big enough for us all to be special on this little earth— except under the sacred canopy of the larger domes of meaning. In Jesus's language, "the branch cut off from the vine is useless" (John 15:5).

II. This Is Us (Our Story)

The next and larger realm of meaning is about Us. This is the dome of our group, our community, our country, our church—perhaps our nationality or ethnic group. For young people, it is often their friends, their gang, or even their kind of music. We seem to need this to contain our own identity and security as social beings. Again, it is both good and necessary. If we do not have a group or, at least, a family with which we can bond, we create asocial beings, sociopaths or psychopaths incapable of bonding anywhere. Most of us have multiple memberships: family, neighborhood, religious affiliation, country. These are our schools for relationship, connection, and almost all virtue as we know it.

Everyone has this level of meaning, consciously or unconsciously, negatively or positively. We are essentially social beings and we live inside of some shared meanings, which become our reference points, our runway. It is the necessary training ground for belonging, attaching, trusting, and loving. If we bond in a healthy family, are proud of our religion and our group possibilities—we might just write new scriptures! Some folks unfortunately just spend their lives defending the boundaries and "glory" of their group. They write programs for war, scapegoating, and major illusion, or at least for smallness. Only group egocentricity is more dangerous than personal egocentricity. It looks like greatness when it is often no more than disguised egotism.

The second dome of meaning gives us myth, cultural heroes, group symbols, flags, special foods, ethnicity, and patriotism. These tell us that we are not alone; we are also connected to a larger story. We might understand that it is fanciful, but it is *shared* meaning and that is important. That we all know the same story of George Washington cutting down the cherry tree is more important than whether it is actually true. But a lot of people stop at the level of shared meaning because it gives a lot more consolation and a lot more security to the small self. In fact, the loyalties at this level have driven most of human history up to now. These identities run so deep that many people have given their lives for their tribe, their country, their religious group. It is one step removed from true transcendence, so it often becomes an easy substitute for God. Watch people and their emotions in regard to war, flag, religion, or team. To die for these feels like dying for God, and that is why it takes so little to talk young people into dying in war.

Men seem especially prone to the consolations of group belonging, perhaps because they are less capable of personal intimacy. Women will die for a child; men prefer to die for a cause. Clearly, we are dealing with archetypal meanings here. If we have not connected with the third level, these are our only gods.

People try to find identity in a group, an institutional affiliation, a nation, a public cause—or, today, like never before, public fame or infamy. Somehow, to be on the news or in social media is to be immortalized. It takes away much of the anxiety of developing a personal self. People feel protected inside of the group identity or public fame. We all connect with one group or another—a Catholic, a Harley-Davidson bike owner, a Chicago Cubs fan—and then sport proud signs about it. It lifts some real burden from our private striving, and there is true comfort in being among our own. Now we don't have to be great by ourselves; we can ride on the coattails of other Polish Americans or other owners of golden retrievers!

A lot of Americans bought into the second level, especially after the World Wars of the twentieth century. It became the operative mythology of this country. How fine to think of the glory of being American. We were the liberators of Europe and the good guys in almost every conceivable context! This romanticized mythology served us very well (although not the rest of the world), until it began to unravel in the 1960s with the Vietnam War, the Civil Rights Movement, the political assassinations, and the hippie movement's wholesale rejection of cultural illusions.

Although deconstruction began in Europe much earlier, it did not really happen in America until the 1960s. Some would date it precisely at 1968. America definitely seems different before and after 1968, and we are still in the process of trying to understand what fell apart and why. Many of my generation think, "It felt so good before, so it must have been right." (American Catholics suffer this on two levels, with the Second Vatican Council ending at about the same time. Thus, there is the terrible temptation to idealize something that once existed, but was also a mixed blessing—just as the present moment is.)

The great This Is Us dome is summed up in that common phrase, "For God and Country." It was engraved above so many lintels, included in the mottos of so many organizations, and placed at the top of so many letterheads in America that most Christians never stopped to realize that it was both heresy and idolatry! Each group, of course, had God all to themselves, just the way our Jewish ancestors wanted to keep God in their Temple, while still daring to call Yahweh, "the Lord of heaven and earth." Tribal gods flourish in second-dome people.

After teaching and observing in churches on six of the seven continents, I am still amazed that Americans are not bothered by the flag in the sanctuary of some of our "catholic" churches. I am also amazed that God tends to look like a banker in Switzerland, a reserved gentleman in England, and a crucified-but-not-resurrected Jesus in fatalistic cultures. We can't see what we can't see. Groupthink ensures a rather total form of blindness. Most women did not consciously recognize the evils of sexism and patriarchy until the 1970s.

In my Kansas childhood, I can honestly say I never heard in our Catholic Church any anti-Protestant sermons or sentiments. We never put them down, we just felt sorry for them! We, like all groups, were comfortable inside our own, self-assured universe. "Their churches are so ugly," we thought. "Why would anyone want to go to those churches, when ours are full of gold, statues, pictures, incense, candles, and color?" Our churches were brimming with meaning—all those stories of saints and miracles. We had apparitions on a regular basis. Mary only appeared to us and never to them. Ours was a totally enchanted world. Theirs was sort of sad and desperate. (Some young Catholics are thinking this way again, unfortunately.)

We never realized, of course, that other children were growing up in their traditions, loving their own worlds just as much as we loved ours—and pitying ours in comparison. Notice all the "us" and "them" language in the above paragraph. That is the way the mind works when it lives primarily under the second dome. It is good and necessary, but finally illusory and dangerous to pitch a tent there.

Catholicism, Americanism, Masonic Lodges, any subculture or mythic system, works like a good joke: We either get it or we don't. If we don't get it, we don't get it. If we *do* get it, we tend to be subsumed beneath its spell—for good or for ill. It becomes a non-rational frame of reference that is hard to shake. I will meet people with PhDs who come to me with the most infantile sense of God or of evil, but that is their childhood myth, still guiding their lives. We normally can't totally change this childhood myth later in life and will usually revert to it in times of crisis or chaos. On the positive side, if we are raised with wonderful mythic stories, which formed us at a deep, archetypal level, we will also return there for sanity and solace. They will be safe containers for the rest of our lives.

The pre-Vatican II "Catholic story" gave us a strong sense of We Are. It was a rather watertight system, as long as it remained isolated and self-assured. This is true today of groups like the Amish, the Mormons, and the Catholics gathering in St. Marys, Kansas. It is much easier to do if we remain autonomous and separate, which is why the entire Law of Holiness (see Leviticus 11–26) and most of the book of Numbers address *how to be separate*. Many people never move beyond this early stage because it provides so much identity and comfort—even though it lacks breadth, depth, and compassion. For many groups, like with early Judaism, separation and holiness are almost identical terms. Jesus, of course, rejects the Law of Holiness in favor of the Law of Universal Compassion. That's a *much* more difficult path: integration rather than separation and segregation.

We must have *commitment-fostering mechanisms* to maintain

life at the second level: symbols, songs, sacred times and places, and, especially, sacrificial things to which we all agree. There is no strong sense of being together in life unless we *do* some things together—especially, it seems, things that are strange, visible, and demand constant sacrificial choice. Wearing black veils almost defines some Arab womanhood— and it works. Not eating meat on Fridays probably made little difference to God, but it sure held us Catholics together. All bowing toward Mecca at the same time is a magnificent cultural practice.

It really works very well, but the trouble is that it feels so godly that *much, if not most, religion is a belonging system more than a search for intimacy with God.* Jesus was not into tribal religion, groupthink, and loyalty tests. Much of the institutional church is into them, however, and always has been. It works too well to call it into question. It holds us together and that feels like salvation, even if it is a very deteriorated form.

God could care less, I'm convinced, but God seems to know that *we* need it. *We* need it so the soul can be settled and trustful, *we* need it to get started, *we* need it for communal encouragement and support. When we knew that *all of us* were eating fish on Friday, that gave us a great sense of group loyalty and sacrifice for a common cause. It gave us a sense of "the heroic" that religion seems to require.

The common experience, however, is that we will need it less and less as we move toward the real Center. Thus, we often see a certain freedom in kind old folks, jubilarian religious, and people who have suffered. In the second half of life, we don't need to be a hero anymore. We just need to be *real*. Augustine put it most daringly: "Love [God] and do what you will"![42]

The more demanding this communal act is, the better it works. The only religions that are growing today are those that ask a lot from their people. The more liberal they are, the more they're falling apart. There are young Hispanic men in New Mexico who are attracted to "no drink, no sex, no gambling" religion much more than to our calm, contemplative, and friendly Catholicism. This is a real problem, because I do believe the second is much more mature and closer to the spirit of Jesus, but we need to understand why Jesus religion normally has to be preceded by John the Baptist religion.

In more ways than we thought, John is the precursor of Jesus.[43] It seems we normally begin conservative (with structure, order, certitude, and absolutes that must eventually fail us), then we move toward more tolerant, risk-taking, exception-granting behavior. Again, we must know the rules before we can break the rules or know what the rules really mean. It is great to start with John the Baptist, but we need to end with Jesus. "No man born of woman is greater than John, but the least born into the Reign of God is better than he" (Matthew 11:11).

III. The Patterns That Are Always True

(The Story: Universal Meaning)

Now let's move to the third and largest dome of meaning, what Peter Berger would call the Sacred Canopy. This is the realm of universal meaning, *The* Story that is always true, the patterns that every culture and religion discover in some manner. This level assures and insures the other two. It holds them together in sacred meaning. This is true transcendence, authentic Spirit, which informs all soul and body work. This is what secularism has rejected. Postmodernism says *there are no* universal narratives that are always true. The cosmic egg is then cracked, because the greatest container is rejected—"and all the king's horses and all the king's men"[44] do not seem capable of putting it back together again. The cosmic egg is uniquely the work of God and healthy religion.

Biblical religion, at its best, honors and combines all three levels: personal journey as raw material, communal identity as school and training ground, and true transcendence as the integration and gathering place for all the parts together. We call it holiness, which is the ultimate form of wholeness. The three great monotheistic religions of Judaism, Islam, and Christianity also make this third level personal. This meaning is not just an idea, but a Person.

Without the great stories that free us from the tyranny and the idolatry of the first two stories, we remain trapped in small cultural and private worlds. Without the great patterns that are always true, we get lost in choosing between tiny patterns. True transcendence frees us from the tyranny of *I Am* and the idolatry of *We Are*. But, if all three are taken seriously, as the Bible does very well, we have a full life—fully human and fully divine.

Some try to fly like Icarus to The Story without journeying through the fumbling and constant humiliations of My Story and Our Story. That's fundamentalism. It looks like passionate religion, but it is not incarnation, it is not biblical, it is not wisdom. It emerged largely in the last century, when we forgot how to read sacred literature and became trapped in very limited notions of how to express truth. Ironically, it seems to indicate a kind of dumbing down of human consciousness, a limiting of meaning so that we can understand it, control it, and always be able to explain it.

Well-educated liberal types, who turn to therapeutic and psychological solutions, tend to get trapped today in the first dome of private meaning and their educated explanations. Thus, they are very prone to individualistic worldviews—my ability to choose, my consciousness, and my freedom are what make an action good, not whether it is really good for society or for the other.

Conservatives tend to get trapped in the second dome of group and tribal loyalties. They desire some common worldview, but then they stop there. Everything is waving the flag of America or the papacy or the Bible or the NRA. In some circles today, you would think we were worshiping the pope instead of Jesus! (It does hold the group together in a time when there is little loyalty to anything. We read in I Samuel 8 how Yahweh gave in to the Jewish demand for a king, even though they were rejecting God in making this request.)

Both progressive thinking and traditional thinking can be a way to avoid the great surrender to God. They have much more to do with personal temperament or needs for control than with any classical spiritual path. To both, *the act of faith will still feel like dying* (to their own constructs and certitudes), and both will find their own excuses to explain away why they should have to "die"—exactly what Jesus did not do.

The person who lives within the total cosmic egg is the mystic, the prophet, the universal human, the saint, the whole one. These are people like Mahatma Gandhi, Saint Bonaventure, Martin Luther King, Jr., Mother Teresa, Saint John Henry

Newman, Dag Hammarskjöld, and Julian of Norwich (my favorite mystic). These are the people who look out—with eyes wide as saucers—at the smaller pictures because they observe from the utterly big picture. These are the ones who can both honor and listen to the little stories and also live in the final state of affairs, already, now. They are often called seers because their perspective contains all the eyes, even, somehow, the eyes of God.

The great ones are beyond mere group loyalties; beyond any simple, dualistic thinking that always puts them on the "right" side; beyond winners and losers, good and bad. Lawrence Kohlberg (1927–1987) would probably have called them Stage 6 people, who live by universal principles while still caring for the specific; honoring cultural norms, yet making room for the exceptions. They have seen in a contemplative way, beyond the shadow and the disguise, beyond the suffocating skin of the private self and the self-serving egotisms of group. Aldous Huxley calls this mystical knowing the Perennial Philosophy. It is the contemplative mind that integrates and gives focus to all our calculating and controlling. Without it, there is only civil and self-serving religion.

However, there will be societal reconstruction. It will come from people who can see in this way. *True reconstruction will be led by those who can see reality at all three levels simultaneously.* They can honor the divine level and live ultimately inside of a great big story line. They will appreciate the needs and context of Our Story and not dismiss it as mere cultural trappings or meaningless traditions. They won't say that My Story is not important either. They won't demean or dismiss people who are working on personal issues or addressing the important identity concerns of the first half of life.

Most importantly, don't think you can separate one from the other. It is not sequential, but simultaneous. Many in our therapeutically focused society think they first must get it together personally and then they will serve groups or search for God. It all happens in a spiral, it seems to me. In fact, there is a natural ecology of checks and balances between the three domes of meaning. I, like many who grew up before deconstruction, was lucky and blessed enough to have good family, religion, and community, and good therapy and time for self-knowledge— overlapping one another like waves from an endless sea. Most people emphasize only one or the other. Think about that, and you will have to agree. Someone who honors all three levels is like a major work of art.

The Need for Boundaries and Limits

Boundaries seem to be the only way that human beings can find a place to stand, a place to begin, a place from which to move out. Even those who think they don't have any boundaries usually do. We discover them when we trespass against them. The human soul has to have face and ground, especially in the first years of life. We can't *begin* liberal. We must begin with some boundaries, givens, criteria, and even absolutes, if for no other reason than to give us a "goad" to kick against (see Acts 26:14).

As Paul belabors in his Letter to the Romans (see especially chapters 2–7), *the Law is given for the sake of information, education, and transformation*, but is not, itself, enlightenment. Even

132

though allegiance to boundaries, limits, and laws is almost universally confused with religion and even salvation itself, "the law will not save anyone" (Galatians 3:11). Law has to do with the pattern of how transformation happens—and that's all. The struggle with boundaries and law creates the wrestling ring, but is not, itself, the encounter or the victory.

Human beings seem to need to fight and engage with something before they can take it seriously—and before they can discover what they really need or want. *The people who never fight religion, guilt, parents, injustice, friends, marriage partners, and laws usually have no deep and free* respect *for their power and importance.* That is probably why we have to begin conservatively, in a certain sense. Any good therapist knows that this is true, as does any cultural anthropologist. The spoiled child, the soft culture, and the entitled adult never produce very much.

It's amazing to me how many creative people have parental or religious goads against which they are still kicking. In fact, it is almost the norm. Adam and Eve, Jacob, Job, Paul, and Mary Magdalene would be scriptural examples. Jesus put it very cleverly, drawing on the psalms: The stone which the builders *reject* is, in fact, the keystone (see Psalm 118:22, Matthew 21:42). Much of the best teaching in the church has emerged precisely in response to condemnations, denials, refusals, rejections, failures, and sin. If we want the best minds in the world to work on an idea, just have Rome condemn it or Washington forbid it. Many of the great saints had at least one difficult parent, including Francis himself. Limits and edges seem to refine things. Shapelessness is just that.

Søren Kierkegaard (1813–1855), the Danish philosopher and theologian, said that the "aesthetic person" and the "moral person" were the most common disguises and avoidances for the truly religious person. A truly religious person, according to Kierkegaard, is someone who makes that scary *leap of faith*, giving up all control and trusting to One they love, rather than safely burying their credit for later redemption (see Matthew 25:14–30). Cult and code feel religious, but they are only the window dressing.

If we are looking for directions for reconstruction, I think we can usually look at *the human need* that conservatives are trying to name. *The way* they express it is usually too righteous and angry and *the rigid solutions* they offer are often elitist, protective of power and the past, but *the need* toward which they are usually pointing is legitimate in some form. People do need some degree of order, predictability, security, and authority in order to begin to function well. We normally need to be John the Baptist before we can be Jesus. The trouble is that most Christians are, in fact, followers of John the Baptist and not Jesus. I had that structure for most of my life, and I still do—which is exactly why I don't need it! It is now, at least in part, internalized and subconsciously operative.

I admit that conservatives often cling to their positions with a reactionary anger that seems unwarranted. They're usually appealing to worst-case scenarios, overreacting to their loss of control, and often fall into group loyalty as a substitute for biblical faith. But give them this much credit: They're saying that human beings need some absolute criteria, some reference points, some givens. We cannot live in constant flux and re-discernment of everything. They are simply asking for the Sacred Canopy!

The psyche cannot live with everything changing every day, everything a matter of opinion, everything relative. We can't build any great civilization when everything is up for grabs. There must be a sound container holding us long enough so we can move beyond survival mode. Most people move into siege mentality and never find time for creativity. Yet, with the information explosion of the past fifty years, many people are moving into greater instability and anxiety, even neurosis.

This probably explains why John Paul II judged it necessary to circle the wagons around Vatican certainties. On the human level, he was undoubtedly right, and God seems to be humble enough to join us there in our need for some certainties. I just don't think it approaches the depth and power of biblical faith. I am not as humble or patient as God is.

There has to be solid ground, trust, and shared security, or we cannot move outward. There has to be a foundational hope, and for hope to be a shared experience there must be agreed-upon meanings and shared stories that excite and inspire us all. If these are truly stories from the great patterns that are always true, they will catapult us into a universal humanity, a pluralistic society, where we can both stand on solid ground and, from that solid ground, create common ground. *If it does not support our movement outward, then it is not solid ground at all.*

This is the difference between a mere loyalist and a great soul. Obedience to norms is not the same as "the obedience of faith" (Romans 1:5). Loyalty to norms prefers order; faith operates in chaos. We need them both because they need one another to work, but the second is more necessary for any creative or new future—and that seems to be where God's Word is always leading us.

The Gift of Confidence

Civilization's greatness has emerged from great minds, creativity, saints, and inventions. Often it emerges, not surprisingly, in periods of disruption and chaos. But greatness also emerges when, above all else, people are *confident*. When we believe—together—that life is good, God is good, and humanity is good, we become very safe and salutary people for others. We do exciting and imaginative things because we are confident that we are part of a story line that is going somewhere, and we want to be connected to something good.

Many people appreciated Kenneth Clark (1903–1983) and his great study of the rise and fall of civilizations. It was made into a popular PBS series some years back. At that time, he said that civilizations emerge as great civilizations precisely when people are confident.[45] In many ways, that's what we lack now. We lack it individually, we lack it corporately, we lack it as a church and as a nation. We are not a confident people. In fact, I'd say the opposite: We suffer an immense lack of confidence that we stand for anything beyond the market, that we *are* anything beyond accidents, or that this is leading to anything good or worthwhile.

The puzzling issue, of course, is how we *create* confidence in a time of no confidence. What are the circumstances that conspire to create a confident era and confident people? Surely those circumstances are so many and so complex that we would call their coming together a "gift of God." We know that we cannot orchestrate a *zeitgeist* on our own.

Theologically speaking, we would say that the virtues of *faith, hope, and love are a participation in the very life of God*. We don't really build up to it; we fall into it. It is not occasioned by perfect circumstances. In fact, most of the people I know who have great faith or hope live in very difficult circumstances. Folks who live in ease, conversely, often have very little faith or hope.

Confidence is really a blending of both faith and hope together. I don't understand the alchemy of that union, but I know when it is present and when it isn't. It often feels like something into which I have accidentally collapsed, something that was given from nowhere, something that is a participation in Someone Else. It is of an entirely different nature than natural virtues like temperance or modesty, which we gain through practice or exercise. I think that is why we pray for hope, wait for it, and believe in it, leaving the ground fallow until it comes. But those who do such things *know* that it does come and is always given—and all they can do is thank Someone.

I think we have to pray at this time for the gift of a shared confidence—that deep, gifted stream that has nothing to do with everything going well, but descends from the heavens like the new Jerusalem, "as beautiful as a bride all dressed for her husband" (Revelation 21:2).

Christian hope is different from optimism. Optimism is a natural virtue and a wonderful gift of temperament when things are going well, when we think tomorrow is going to be better than today. Christian hope has nothing to do with the belief that tomorrow is necessarily going to be better than today. The bride is present and that is enough reason for a foundational happiness, even if all else is falling apart. Jesus seems to be saying that if even one mustard seed is sprouting, or one dime found, or one sheep recovered (see Luke 15)—that is enough reason for a big party! Even a small indicator of God is still an indicator of God—and therefore an indicator of reason, meaning, and final joy. A little bit of God goes a long way.

Six

Cleaning Our Lenses

In order to reconstruct, we need to be open to something more than cerebral, rational knowing. We need to move toward a more spacious, contemplative knowing. We need to move beyond the dualistic, seesawing mind that makes quick judgments, beyond the self and its own self-interest, beyond win/lose and either/or worldviews. This is actually conversion in its most basic sense, but it is also the way to enormous wisdom and the vision of God. Only the whole self is ever ready for the whole God.

There are many ways of "knowing" reality. Others might use different or broader descriptions, but I'm going to describe seven ways here. By *ways* of knowing I mean *how* we come to see what we see. This topic was traditionally the beginning course for all studies in philosophy and went by the word *epistemology*. It was the first philosophy course we seminarians took. We had to reflect on *how* we knew, before we could clearly see *what* we knew, which was called metaphysics. We had to recognize our own lenses and biases before we described what we saw, or we could not trust what we said we saw.

Even if the word *epistemology* is no longer a well-known word, the clarity that it offers is needed more than ever because we have many lenses, most of which are largely unowned and unacknowledged. To be honest, Buddhists tend to focus on awareness of these lenses more than most Christians today, especially since humility and detachment are no longer virtues much admired in the West. Early stage religion *must* be about cleaning these lenses, as Teresa of Ávila says about the first room in the Interior Castle. Otherwise, we are not able to move forward to other rooms.

I could never adequately treat the seven ways of knowing in this brief chapter, but I will describe them in quick, surely over-simplified form. More than anything else, I hope to help you clean your own lenses so you can really take in the message of this book and, more importantly, the gospel. Like all stories on conversion and transformation, we must begin by admitting that we need a whole new head! It will take major surgery to cut off the old head, which we thought was the only one.

Our culture developed a sharp split between rational knowing and every other kind of knowing. The first was considered superior and legitimate knowing; all others were suspect.

Intellect

The lens that we most associate with knowing is *intellectual* knowing. It's the result of education, and formal education in particular. It has to do with science, reason, logic, and what we call intelligence. Today, it is also common to speak of left-brain knowledge: knowing facts, figures, and information. It's a good way to know. We're grateful for it. Most of us are trained to think that it is the only way of knowing or the superior way of knowing. Yet that isn't necessarily true. Seeing intellectual intelligence as the best or only way of knowing is actually a great limitation. Daniel Goleman's groundbreaking book, *Emotional Intelligence*,[46] has demonstrated this in a rather convincing way. In fact, mere intellectual gray matter is often an actual liability in the "real world."

The "absent-minded professor," the "nerd," and the "academic" are contemporary terms indicating people with this now-apparent limitation. Yet, during my time in the seminary (1950s–1960s), this was the attribute for which we were most trained, most admired, and most ordained—even among Franciscans, who should have known better! For the most part, we were trained to be academics, not pastoral workers. We learned Latin and Greek to connect with ideas and the past, not Spanish or native languages to help us connect with actual people now. Intellectual knowing has all sorts of biases, but never needs to own them because it thinks of itself as so "smart."

Will

The second way of knowing is *volitional* knowing. That's the kind of knowing that comes from making choices, commitments, and decisions, then sticking with them, and experiencing them at different stages. Anyone who has made and then kept vows knows what I'm talking about. The reason people marry and the reason people stay married are not the same reason. In fact, reasons can change each year, perhaps even each month. It's the same for those of us who keep religious vows. The reason we first take them and the reason we continue in vows changes as we grow. It is a knowing that comes from making choices and the very process of struggling with the choices.

This knowing is a kind of cumulative knowing that emerges over time. It is the experiential knowing that comes from staying in the trenches over a period of choices, disillusionments, and re-choosings. It is closer to wisdom than mere informational knowledge, but is not, of itself, wisdom. We might choose and re-choose for some very bad or inferior motives. We might decide out of fear, anger, or vengeance. This is *willful* knowing (coming from the ego-driven agenda), as opposed to *willing* knowing (coming from surrender and trust). Gerald May (1940–2005) understands and explains these two different kinds of will brilliantly.[47] Like no other author I know, he puts together spirituality with very good psychology, without sacrificing either.

Examine your own life. Maybe you made a decision and, after you made the decision, you began to view reality differently. You look out from a new viewpoint. The marriage decision is probably the biggest one for most people, but there are certainly many others. To what lifestyle will you aspire? Where will you live? What type of work will you do happily? After making conscious decisions in these big areas, you ask different questions of life. You taste reality at a different level. You will "know" in a new and potentially insightful way.

To have decided for something at ever-deeper levels of free choice is to be a grounded and, usually, a very alive person. The Franciscan Blessed John Duns Scotus (1266–1308) felt that volitional knowing, will, was actually higher and closer to love than intellectual knowing. This always distinguished the Franciscan school from the Dominican Thomists, who gave a primacy to knowledge. I am a Scotist because John Duns Scotus was building on Francis's primacy of love over knowledge.

Emotion

Until very recently, emotional knowing had not been appreciated by the intelligentsia, nor by the church in many ways.

As mentioned above, Daniel Goleman demonstrates that it is helpful to have both a good IQ and a good EQ (emotional quotient). In fact, if we have to choose between the two, EQ is a higher indicator of success in life, job, and relationships than IQ!

Great emotions are especially powerful teachers. I'm so aware of this in the experience of grief, after experiencing the deaths of my mother, a teenage niece, and my father. Even anger and rage are great teachers, if we listen to them. They have so much power to reveal our deepest self to ourselves and to others, yet we tend to consider them negatively. Yes, they are dangerous and often totally rearrange how we know—or if we know—reality at all. No wonder many even think of anger as a sin.

Believe it or not, such emotions are ways of knowing. They have the capacity to blind us, but also the power to open us up and bring us to profound conversion, humility, and honesty. People who are too nice and never suffer or reveal their own negative emotions, usually do not know very much about themselves—and so the rest of us do not take them too seriously. Consider if that is not true in your own circle of relationships.

I would guess that people die and live much more for emotional knowing than they ever will for intellectual, rational knowing. Rational knowing really converts no one. If rational knowing is the superior kind, religion has set itself up for major problems. No wonder atheism has emerged as a unique problem in the rational West.

In the past, when people told me about the death of a parent or a loved one, I listened to them and thought I understood them. After I personally had to walk through encounters with death and experienced this new emotion called grief, I henceforth have lived in a whole new house. I'm in a different space than I have experienced before.

We have found that grief work is an essential and central part of men's work. Almost all male initiations had to lead men into grief, where they are not at home at all. The feminist movement, however, has rightly recognized that many women have to be led into a necessary anger. Men in our culture consciously avoid the powerlessness of grief; women consciously avoid the unpleasantness of anger. Both denials trap emotions in the unconscious, where they do their dirty work indirectly. We need to know, feel, own, and find appropriate expression for our negative as well as our positive emotions.

Love, ecstasy, hatred, jealousy, fear, despair, anguish: each have their lessons. To taste these emotions is to live in a new reality afterward, with a new ability to connect. We can all tell when someone has emotional knowledge of a thing, as opposed to mere head knowledge.

Many in America have spoken about being out of touch with or disconnected from an emotional life. This is always a prelude to further problems, or at least a significant loss of contact with reality.

On a trip to India, I twice heard the same quote: "There are no atheists in India." It's not surprising that many of the temple services were also filled with groaning, tears, sensuous dance, waving hands, and ecstatic prostrations. We had best not call such religious experiences merely emotional, especially when we see an exodus to the charismatic and Pentecostal forms of Christianity. The feelings also can, and must, know God. I fear that many of my seminary professors are going to be wallflowers in the great dance of heaven. They will have nothing to figure out anymore, only a party to join.

Senses

Bodily or sensory knowing comes through the senses, by touching, moving, smelling, seeing, hearing, breathing, tasting—and especially at a deep or unconscious level. Becoming aware of our senses in a centered way allows us to awaken, to listen, to connect. It allows us to know reality more deeply, on our body's terms instead of only on our brain's terms.

I once gave a yoga retreat in which I talked and a friend, Jim Reale, led the participants in body and breath experiences connected with what I had just said. I felt the message went far deeper than usual, and the prayer had a reality to it that was grounded and heartfelt. Maybe all my retreats should be yoga retreats, yet that very word would scare many Christians away. Many of us prefer it all to remain in the head, where it is non-threatening and we have control over agreeing or disagreeing.

We sometimes speak of "kinesthetic knowing," which might be available to a dancer or long-distance runner, and "corporeal knowing," in the context of childbirth and lovemaking. In fact, the Hebrew language describes lovemaking as "knowing" the other person.

Many teachers of contemplative prayer find that breathing exercises are the surest way for some people to know God in their bodies. It is no surprise that Jesus touched most people he healed. Something very different is communicated and known through physical touch, in contrast with what is communicated through mere words. Strange that there is much more

New Testament evidence for the washing of feet as a sacrament than for Holy Orders, but we deemphasized the mandated foot-washing (in John 13:15) in favor of Holy Orders—and, until recently, the bishop even wore white gloves when he performed ordinations!

In my early days in Albuquerque, I could look out the front window of my hermitage to where we had constructed a seven-circuit labyrinth, with seven 180-degree turns—a turn each time faced an arm of the cross laid out on the ground. One day, a middle-aged Franciscan who was making a directed retreat with me was walking it quite deliberately. When I walked out to talk to him afterward, he had tears in his eyes that he did not understand. The very walking led him to a knowing too deep for words. That's when tears take over. Tears were called a gift of the Holy Spirit by many of the ancient teachers in the church, especially the Syrian Fathers. They are surely a deep entranceway into knowing that is both cleansing and softening. Tradition tells us that one of the Syrian fathers said that we do not know God until we have wept.

Images

Next, there is imaginative or imaginal knowing. Imaginal knowing is the only way that the unconscious can move into consciousness. It happens through fantasy, through dreams, through symbols, where all is "thrown together" (*sym-ballein* in Greek). It happens through pictures, events, and well-told stories. It happens through poetry, where well-chosen words create an image that, in turn, creates a new awareness—that was in us already. We knew it, but we didn't know it. It was in the unconscious, as we say, and needed to be pulled forth. It seems that the right brain and the unconscious do not know conceptually, but through images. Thus, people will often break into tears when seeing a picture, a movie, or a human event, much more often than when having an idea.

In the Catholic tradition, we have a strong sense of the sacramental nature of the world. We know spiritual things by analogy, metaphor, symbol, and sign. In fact, it is the only way that we can know spiritual reality. Moses must be shielded when God passes by because God can only be known indirectly (Exodus 33:18–23).

Perhaps the Achilles' heel of Protestant theology, largely owing to the period of history in which it emerged, is that it tries to find truth far too much in words, preaching, and correct ideas. No wonder that there are now at least five thousand Protestant denominations—and growing. Words are simply too brittle, narrow, and culturally limited to ever be a broad or solid basis for unity. As I recall, C. G. Jung believed literalism is the death of the religious instinct. That is certainly true.

We must be open to imaginal knowing because this work of reconstruction is not going to be done logically, rationally, or cerebrally. That mode of knowing is simply not adequate to the greatness and the depth of the task. Once we touch the way people *imagine a situation*, change will happen easily and naturally. That is why Jesus told stories to help people *re-imagine* their lives and their relationship with the universe. Once the overall gestalt switches, thinking and feeling change almost immediately.

Once, a Vietnam veteran who had been decorated for killing

many innocent people in Vietnam came to me in tears after seeing a dead body in a ditch. Thirty years later, he got it—not through thousands of sermons, but through a reconfigured and remembered image of the horror of death. Maybe all true knowing is *re-membering*, putting the members and memories together in a new and now significant story.

We can't control or manufacture these images. We have to allow the images to show themselves. As Teresa of Ávila put it, there are at least two wells in the life of prayer. The first well we have to dig ourselves and keep the trenches flowing toward it. For the second and better well, we just wait until water bubbles up.[48] That's contemplation, where we get the false self out of the way and the gift shows itself like an apparition.

These gifts from the second well have a more personal character. They are usually attached to a symbol and filled with unexplainable energy. They seldom take the form of a verbal locution or clear concept. Thus, there is a common need for a guide, a teacher, an interpreter of dreams at this level. It's also why one picture or poem or gnarl of a tree can blow us away when we are truly centered or at prayer.

In some ways, we taught sacramental theology, but the truly sacramental is, in fact, scary and inherently in God's hands. In a sense, we tried to limit God to Seven Sacraments and clearly defined all the hows, whens, whos, and wheres. A sacramental way of life can and will really change us, but most of us don't really want to go into the unknown. It is no surprise that we have avoided images in favor of concepts, personal faith journeys in favor of well-defined sacraments. The "tabernacle" of Exodus was on the move, leading the people through the desert. Now the tabernacle must, by order of Canon Law (#938),[49] be *immovable*, that is, be nailed or bolted down. What a different idea!

It is interesting to me that iconoclasm (the destruction of images) was a central issue in two major schisms within church history: in the East in the eighth and ninth centuries, and in the West at the time of the Reformation. Protestantism has never totally recovered from such left-brain fury. We know we are dealing with something archetypal and powerful when the human psyche reacts to such a violent degree. Catholics probably kept images domesticated by the mass production of sentimental, saccharine, and anglicized images of all the great mysteries. Perhaps we killed the imaginal mind by pretending to honor it.

Aesthetic

That leads us to the next distinct kind of knowing. In some ways, aesthetic knowing is the most attractive, but I think it's the least converting. Aesthetic knowing is often either so pretty or so ugly that we tend to stop there. Art in all its forms so engages us and satisfies us that many go no deeper. Because they've been exposed to the picture or the poem or the wonderful piece of sculpture, the aesthete and the dilettante think that, in fact, they've changed their lives or experienced true transcendence. Usually aesthetic knowing is only an entranceway, but it is indeed a way of knowing too.

This art-for-art's-sake attitude was part of the reason for the needed reaction of the Protestant reformers. Just take a tour of the "gilded lily" churches of Europe—paintings from floor to ceiling and monuments to bishops and popes. I cannot imagine this centering anyone on God or on anything except, "Aren't we wonderful." Baroque and Rococo churches were supposed to bring people back to Catholicism. They might well have done that, but I doubt whether they brought them back to the gospel. Aesthetics don't always demand transformation or increase real knowing, and often become a seductive substitute for the same. Thus, we have the revealing words *connoisseur* (from the French for knowing "thoroughly"), or *dilettante* (from the Italian for an amateur who thinks he or she is not), or an *epicurean* who thinks that "the best" is, in fact, the best.

People who espouse aesthetic knowing play around superficially with profound ideas and beauty, but they may never move toward substance. Aesthetic knowing never hits their politics. It never changes their attitude toward the poor. It is all posturing and posing. Aesthetics can be a way of knowing, but it can also be an avoidance of knowing. Picasso's *Guernica* told us something profound about the evil of violence. The popular 1994 movie *Pulp Fiction*, conversely, trivializes, normalizes, and cheapens the evil of violence.

Image can get in the way of substance. Ritual can be an avoidance of reality, as the Mass itself sometimes has become. The Japanese people seem seldom to ask questions of metaphysics or religion, yet they are some of the most highly ritualized people in the world. Good and ubiquitous ritual can dull and substitute for the authentic religious drive.

Still, aesthetic knowing is a central and profound way of knowing. Maybe it is open to misuse precisely because it is so powerful. I've seen art lead to true changes of consciousness. I have seen people change their lives in response to a novel, a play, a piece of music, or a movie like *Dead Man Walking*. Their souls were prepared, and God got in through the right metaphor at the right time. They saw their own stories clarified inside of a larger story line.

Epiphany

The last way of knowing, which I'd think religion would prefer and encourage, is epiphanic knowing. An epiphany is a parting of the veil, a life-changing manifestation of meaning, the *eureka* of awareness of self and the Other. It is the radical grace, which we cannot manufacture or orchestrate. There are no formulas which ensure its appearance. It is always a gift, unearned, unexpected, and larger than our present life.

Epiphany happens in unusual settings, usually non-religious settings, which is often a needed sign that we didn't cause it ourselves by devotion or morality. I have met very few people who have had their great conversions inside churches or during liturgies, for example. We cannot manufacture epiphanies. We can only ask for them, wait for them, expect them, know they are given, keep out of the way, and thank Someone afterward.

PART TWO

Finding a Third Way

Prayer for Presence

Let us be present to the now. It's all we have and it's where God will always speak to us. The now holds everything, rejects nothing and, therefore, can receive God too. Help us, God, to be present to the place we most fear, because it always feels empty, it always feels boring, it always feels like it's not enough. Help us find some space within that we don't try to fill with ideas or opinions. Help us find space so you, loving God, can show yourself in that place where we are hungry and empty. Keep us out of the way, so there is always room enough for you.

Good God, we believe that you are here and your presence gives us hope. We thank you for each day of our lives. We thank you for so many further chances to understand, to forgive again, to trust again, and to love. We thank you that we live now, that our problems are soul-sized. We ask that you teach us and lead us, that you put the thoughts into our mind that you want us to think, the feelings in our hearts that you want us to feel. Reconstruct us. Put us together because we don't know how to do it ourselves. We trust that you are hearing this prayer, and that you care for the answer more than we do. We pray therefore not alone, but with the whole body of Christ in Jesus's name. Amen.

Seven

What Is Your Window on Reality?

Everybody looks at the world through their own lens, a matrix of culturally inherited qualities, family influences, and other life experiences. This lens, or worldview, truly determines what we bring to every discussion. When Jesus spoke of the coming of the Reign of God, he was trying to change people's foundational worldview. When Francis spoke of his marriage to Lady Poverty, he was using a lovely metaphor to describe his central thesis for life. When Americans speak of money as "the bottom line," they are revealing more about their real worldview than they realize.

We would do well to get in touch with our own operative worldview. It is there anyway, so we might as well know what this highly influential window on reality is. It's what really motivates us. Our *de facto* worldview determines what catches our attention and what we don't notice at all. It's largely unconscious and yet it drives us to do this and not that. It is surely important to become conscious of such a primary lens or we will never know what we *don't* see and why we see other things out of all perspective.

Until we can allow the gospel to move into that deepest level of the unconscious and touch our operative worldviews, nothing substantial is going to change. It will only be rearranging the furniture, not constructing a new room. Conversion is about constructing a new room, or maybe even a whole new house.

I wonder if this was not the full meaning of Jesus's words to Francis from the cross at San Damiano: "Rebuild my house, for you see that it is falling into ruins."

I remember the first time I was on an extended hermitage in Kentucky. When I was walking a little path, one of the recluses came walking toward me. Now, the recluses are more hermits than hermits! They only come out from their seclusion for events like Holy Week and Christmas—and all the monks are waiting to see if they are glowing or crazy! I knew who this hermit was. I'd heard of him as a former abbot. I was excited that I would get to see this holy man, and I didn't want to break his reclusiveness, so I said nothing. But he apparently knew I was on the grounds. He said to me, as he pointed upward, "Richard, when you preach, be sure to keep telling the people, '*God is not out there!*' Thank you." And then he went on down the path.

That recluse had the worldview that I would call truly Christian: Incarnational. It is actually not too common, even among baptized Christians. The vast majority of Christians I have met worldwide are actually theists, but not Incarnational at all. God is still *out* there, invited *into* things, and they are all inviting God to come *to* them. Theism, the most common form of religion, is still a split worldview. True Christianity is totally integrative. There is one world, all supernatural, and God comes *through* us, not to us. It is imaged by Paul as the body of Christ and by John as the vine and the branches. Jesus speaks of "one flock and one shepherd" (John 10:16), "abiding in love" (John 15:10), or "I and the Father are one" (John 10:30).

So few people have experienced this divine image as the innermost possession of their own souls. Christ only meets them from without, never from within, so their operative worldview is still, "God is out there and we are down here," a three-level universe: Hell, Earth, and Heaven. It is always a matter of getting God down here and getting us up there. Actually, many, if not most, of the orations in the official *Sacramentary* (prayers for Catholic Eucharist) still reveal this split worldview. Unfortunately (in this case), *lex orandi est lex credendi*: The way we pray shapes the way we believe.

Our operative worldview is formed by three images that are inside every one of us. They are not something from outside; they have already taken shape within us. All we can do is become aware of them, which is to awaken them. The three images to be awakened and transformed are our image of self, our image of God, and our image of the world. A true hearing of the gospel transforms those images into a very exciting and, I believe, truthful worldview. When we say Christ is the truth, that's what we mean. Christ renames reality correctly, according to what reality honestly is, putting aside whatever we think it is or whatever we fear it is. Reality is always better than any of us imagined or feared; there is joy associated with a true hearing of the gospel.

Normally, our worldview answers several foundational questions. The first question is: "What should be?" or "What's the grand and final vision?" That, in great part, is what we've lost: what should be, what it could be, and what the world is supposed to mean. We're almost afraid to believe what should be. We deny, or at least doubt, all aspirational shoulds and oughts.

The second has to do with the state of things: "Why are things messed up?" or "Why do we suffer?" or "Why are things not the way they should be?" The earliest religions credited this to fussy gods, demanding gods, punishing gods, or even toxic gods. God, in general, was not someone to be liked. The world, furthermore, was a dangerous place, filled with dangerous spirits. That left the individual self-insecure, fearful, and pleading.

The third question that our worldview answers is: "How do we get from what's broken to what should be?" or "How do we live to make things right?" or, quite simply, "What does it mean to be a good human being?"

All together, we could put it this way: "What should life be?" "Why isn't it?" "How do we repair it?" When these are answered for us, at least implicitly, we have our game plan and we can live safely and with purpose in this world. Without this game plan, our life is a bad novel with no beginning, middle, or end; circular, but not a spiral.

Differing worldviews have their own explanations for suffering and their own ways of trying to resolve it. Some early peoples felt that the explanation for suffering was simply imposition of trials and threats by a fussy and temperamental god. Somehow, we had to get this god on our side by sacrificing a virgin daughter or an eldest son, perhaps by burning them at the stake. We see remnants of this in the story of Abraham and Isaac. Somehow, suffering and sacrifice were supposed to please an angry god. Often, people felt they had to demean or punish themselves to get God to stop punishing them. Literally, they had to beat God to the punch. Many contemporary people have not moved much beyond this worldview. It is a sort of sadomasochistic game of reward and punishment that still lurks deep in the unconscious of many churchgoing Christians.

The Buddhist worldview would say we suffer because we have too much desire. Spirit is imprisoned inside vicious matter and we must move beyond matter to spirit. The Buddhist goal is Nirvana, freedom from matter, freedom from desire. The solution is meditation, so that we see the truth. Of course, they've got something very right. We need to move beyond the shadow and the disguise, something we in the West have not learned very well. For the most part, we've avoided the deeper forms of transformative prayer. One of Buddhism's great insights is demonstrated in leading its people to that deeper form of prayer which dislodges the ego and changes the agenda-driven person. Prayer is not just asking God for things.

The Marxist worldview blames suffering on private property, rich people, and greed. There is some truth to that, but Marxism carries it to extremes. The Marxist expounds universal equality through enforced common ownership of all possessions. Once we accept that, we read everything through those eyes. This worldview does address some problems of injustice and inequality, but it creates new ones. Those who have are judged as bad; those who have not are automatically superior. This divides the good and bad people neatly, but it just isn't that simple. Nor can "virtue" be enforced; if it is enforced, it is not virtue.

The capitalist worldview is a little closer to home for most who might be reading this book. We don't think of capitalism as something to criticize. Yet capitalism offers its own explanations that are less than Christlike. The capitalist worldview blames suffering on inertia and laziness. Those who are lazy and irresponsible do not achieve capitalism's goal: material prosperity. That's why most analyses in the media are economic analyses. "How's the economy doing?" That's our big question, because materialism is our basic mythology. What quickly follows from this worldview is "every person for themselves" and an almost necessary lack of compassion for those left behind. Once competition and success are virtues, not to be competitive or successful is almost sinful.

The postmodern and liberal worldview would say the reason we suffer is that we're uptight, that there are too many laws and structures. If there were unlimited freedom for everybody to be true to their deepest feelings and instincts, we'd have a wonderful world. The solution therefore is to rebel and be true to myself: "If it feels good, do it" or "I must find myself and take care of myself before I can worry about others." The trouble is that people with these concerns never get to others because the ego is insatiable. Yet, this worldview remains largely uncriticized in the sophisticated West.

When we describe these worldviews as crassly as I just did, they sound absurd. Perhaps that can open us to listen to what Jesus says about worldview, because Jesus is turning our common worldviews upside-down. He is giving us a different story line for the understanding of what reality means. This change of story lines, this switch of plots, is at the foundation of all true conversions and, therefore, of all genuine reconstruction.

Getting in Touch with Your Worldview

It will probably not be easy for you to name your operative worldview objectively. It's the grid of your deepest experience.

Your operative worldview is not largely the product of rational or deliberate choice. You absorb it from your parents, from your first years of life, and from your formative years in general. In some cases, it is altered by a deeply influential person, book, or experience.

It's true that even the most enlightened people see the world from a certain, defined cultural perspective. But they also see beyond their own biases to something transcendent, something that crosses the boundaries of culture and individual experience. People with a distorted image of self, world, or God will be largely incapable of experiencing what is really real in the world. They will see things through a narrow keyhole. They'll see instead what they need reality to be, what they're afraid it is, or what they're angry for it being. They'll see everything through their anger, their fear, or their agenda. In other words, they won't see *it* at all.

That's the opposite of the contemplative, who sees what is, whether it's favorable or not, whether it meets his needs or not, whether she likes it or not, and whether or not that reality causes weeping or rejoicing. Most of us will usually misinterpret our experience until we have been moved out of our false center. Until then, there is too much of the self in the way. Most of us do not see things as they are; we see things as *we are*. That is no small point.

Dennis, Sheila, and Matthew Linn have written a beautiful book called *Good Goats*[50] that helps us see how many people are trapped by counterproductive and even destructive images of God. When we touch our deepest image of self, a deeper image of reality, or a new truth about God, we're touching something that opens us to the sacred. We'll want to weep or to be silent, or to run away from it and change the subject because it's too deep, it's too heavy. As T. S. Eliot (1888–1965) wrote in *Four Quartets*, "human kind cannot bear very much reality."[51]

When we tamper with these images, we are changing our own compass and the coordinates of our reality. That's what the Catholic Church dared to do at the Second Vatican Council. In a major way, the Council told Roman Catholics of the twentieth century to renew our images of God, of worship, and of the very nature of Catholicism, and to return to a much more scripturally based foundation.

After every Council since the beginning of the Church, there has been a major schism, a major split, except after Vatican II. We feel we're horribly split into liberals and conservatives, but no formal schism has taken place. I think the problem now is that this generation can't handle much more psychic change. I don't think it can handle any more liberal changes that will redefine established patterns. When the psyche is in such a state of disarray and confusion as it is today, it longs for and desperately needs some givens, some absolutes. To again quote T. S. Eliot, it needs "a still point of the turning world."[52]

That's why my colleagues and I emphasize contemplation. It's the way of going to the experience of the absolute without going toward ideology. Do you see the difference? It's going toward the experience of the good, the true, and the beautiful without going into a head trip, or taking the small self too seriously, or taking one's momentary vantage point too seriously either:

> Neither from nor towards; at the still point, there the dance is . . .

Where past and future are gathered. Neither movement
from nor towards,

Neither ascent nor decline. Except for the point, the still
point,

There would be no dance, and there is only the dance.[53]

Worldview as Matrix of God-image, Self-image, World-image

The God-image, the self-image, and the world-image are deeply connected. Normally, when one of them changes, the other two have to readjust. So, when our God-image changes, then *we* have to change. When our world-image is adjusted, we are confused or even depressed for a while. That's why theology and philosophy were called the king and queen of sciences. In a classic university, all students had to examine these fields or it was not a *uni*-versity (with one center).

For example, if our God is a judge, then we will remain fearful little children. If, suddenly, God becomes love, we have to learn how to be in love. We have to change. We become the God we worship, as so many have said. We can pretty much assess what a person is like and sense what their God is like. If they're fear-filled, we know what their God-image is.

Another example is easy to find today: practical agnosticism. Unlike atheism, which denies God, practical agnosticism simply says, "I don't know, and I don't care." Yet that, too, is an organizing principle. If "I don't know, and I don't care" is a *centralizing image*, boundaries soon evaporate. There's nothing really demanded, nothing really expected, nothing really needed, nothing really called forth. We just move wherever the ego leads us. Agnosticism amounts to a disorganizing principle rather than organizing anything.

We can see from these examples that when one image changes, the others will change as well. If we want to grow in these areas, we need to honestly bring our operative images of self and God to conscious consideration. It might even be good to journal about this over a period of time. Avoid the temptation to be fashionable or socially acceptable, like merely saying, "My God is love." Don't write it down until it is a felt experience. Let's be honest.

There are a lot of us who are still operating from the inadequate or even toxic images of God we learned as children. For example, we're afraid we're going to be shamed because our early experience of religion was largely of God as police officer. Our image of God will improve as we learn more about God. If it is really God we are meeting, it will only get better. Take that as absolute.

Attachment to Self-image

Let me give you some possible images of self to examine—always remembering that you must have a self-image, and it is best to have a positive but honest one. The only real problem is your *attachment* to that self-image. That is what can become a kind of chosen blindness.

In general, look for both an adjective and a noun in these personal self-descriptions: realistic intellectual, ineffective dreamer, convinced Christian, hardworking mother, for example. Be careful when the terms are too positive or too grandiose, because they usually come from what is externally admired rather than what you really are or even want to be. Also, be careful when they're too negative because you have to live down to them. Note that might be exactly what you are doing: "living up to" or "living down in," instead of living who you *are* in God.

Let's say you think of yourself as a positive homemaker. This self-image says, "I'm always positive, I'm always upbeat, and always optimistic." That's fine; there's no good or bad to any of these. But, if you are too attached to it, you lock yourself into a self-image and then see everything through a distorted lens. You will not be able to see when you are *not* this way, although almost everyone else will! One way to tell if you've gone too far is to consider what offends you. If you are hurt when other people do not respond immediately to your cheery housecleaning, then perhaps you've over-identified with the homemaker image. If you are threatened by women who do housekeeping differently, you are too invested in your own nest. Is this not many of the people we all know?

Who-you-are-in-God, or *love*, takes no offense (1 Corinthians 13:5). The True Self is an indestructible image, as opposed to the "heap of broken images" that Eliot calls the modern Waste Land.[54] An honest self-image needs neither to be asserted nor defended. It just is, and it is enough. Thus, the saints speak of "resting" in God. Only the True Self can rest. The false self is inherently restless.

Some other common self-images include unhappy child, strong leader, enlightened feminist, poor student, organized manager, gregarious friend. None of these is bad or good. The only problem is your attachment to them.

Look especially for images of dominance or submission in role, intelligence, age, race, class, gender, or family of origin.

Too much one-sidedness in either direction is usually an indication of the false self. What is it that holds you fast? What's your trap? What is it you have to live up to? That's your enslaving self-image. The saint needs neither to dominate nor to grovel, but can do either if the moment rightly calls for it. The holy person is thus the ultimately free person. If you *need* to dominate, you are not free to *not* dominate, and that is not freedom for you or anybody else.

In the spiritual journey, you will naturally detach from self-images as you draw closer to God. In God's presence, you don't need to stand on your self-image or project your self-image. In truth, your overly clad self is what keeps you from God and from other people. To be present with God, you will gradually become very transparent and vulnerable; you will gradually let go of roles, titles, masks, and identities. They are all in the way. God's perfect loving of you makes it possible to shed your "character armor" (à la Ernest Becker [1924–1974][55]), just as with a true friend. I suspect this is the archetypal fascination of lovers undressing one another or undressing themselves for the other. That's very powerful stuff, and not just titillation.

If I'm overly self-identified as a realistic intellectual, then God has to appear as the realistic intellectual, because that's who I am. God can't come as the humble little man on welfare and speak to me because I can't hear him. If I am over-identified as moral and law-abiding, I wonder how I would ever meet the God of mercy and forgiveness, which seems to be God's very name. When God always has to come in our preferred form, then we are in charge, and God is no longer God, or we will meet a very small part of God.

One of the great graces of growing older is that people often start to let go of spurious and self-serving images. Perhaps the reason for a mid-life crisis is that God is trying to help us let go of our attachment to being a doctor, a priest, a mother, or whatever we think we are. Part of the great conversion experience is precisely the ecstatic recognition that "I am not who I *think* I am." It can be a very terrifying thing, even though it is the ultimate liberation. If we have entirely identified with one persona in our 20s, 30s, and 40s, we just can't imagine what we would be without it—which is exactly the problem.

The spiritual life is always about letting go of unnecessary baggage so that we're prepared for death's final letting go. That can only happen if we're willing to know that our self-image is not the deepest self. Self-image is an important and good part of the journey, and it might even have helped us to taste moments of the I Am—but there's much more. Finally, like Paul, "it is no longer I, but Christ living in me" (Galatians 2:20). My deepest me is God.

A Growing Image of World/Reality

Our operative world-image is finally our "realm," that which is real for us and becomes the organizing principle that situates our daily decisions, lifestyle choices, and ultimate sense of direction and significance. It tends to grow, but also is founded in very early and largely non-rational teachings, at our mother's knee and by our father's example. I knew that the world could be trusted, for example, by the time I was in kindergarten. At least, that is when I first remember thinking that way. Probably I *knew* it by three, because I could trust both Mom and Dad.

How do you really see the world? Thomas Jefferson and George Washington, like most of the founding fathers of our country, were deists, similar to those theists I talked about earlier. They weren't Christian in the real sense of the term. Deists believe that the universe is like a clock, wound up by God and left ticking along without God's further intervention. For the deist, "God is in his heaven—all's right with the world."[56] Certainly God has no active caring or providential guidance for this world. An inner kind of logic is unfolding, and God is watching it. If God does step in, it is probably just to punish, which sounds much like the emotionally unavailable father that most people seem to have had in history. Many Americans who go to church regularly are still deists in every practical sense.

Another image of the world includes power and struggle as the bottom line. We used to hear the world described as a veil of tears, an obstacle course, a bunch of hoops for us to jump through. Reality is basically oppositional, testy, antagonistic. Many ancient peoples, especially before the person of Jesus, saw the world as a heroic contest. Just read Germanic and Viking myths, and others of peoples from harsh climates. It's very understandable: Their physical world naturally became their world-image. We seldom find such harsh and dour world-images among Polynesian islanders or Sicilian fishermen.

Then there's the perspective that everything's planned, that there's no freedom to God or to the self, that we're just puppets. This is the language of fate, karma, destiny, and the eternal plan of God. Fundamentalist language very often sounds like that, without much room for God to break *our interpretation* of God's own rules. Yet the biblical tradition had a strong, daring sense of free will, acknowledging both the freedom of God and the freedom of the self. We would do well not to lose that sense of freedom. From an utterly free God come the central mysteries of forgiveness, mercy, providence, and election— which, by definition, are God breaking God's own rules, and always in our favor. How wonderful!

How about the world as survival of the fittest? Or "life is just a bowl of cherries"? Or the view summed up in the terrible bumper sticker, "Life's a bitch and then you die." Why would people sport such a bumper sticker unless part of them believes it? They had best be aware of the glasses they wear. *How* you see is *what* you will see.

In looking at your world-image, look especially for any hints of purpose or direction, meaning or plan—or lack of it. Sit alone in the silence today and ask, "What do I expect of life? What do I owe life? What does the world offer me? What do I offer the world?" That will pretty much reveal your operative world-image. Is the universe for you or against you? Is it a hostile universe or are there angels in every tree?

Eight

The Great Chain of Being

Francis called all creatures, no matter how small, by the name of brother and sister, because he knew they had the same source as himself.

BONAVENTURE

I would like to reclaim an ancient, evolving, and very Franciscan metaphor to rightly name the nature of the universe, God, and the self, and to direct our future thinking: the image of the Great Chain of Being.

Through this image, Scholastic theologians tried to communicate a linked and coherent world.[57] The essential and unbreakable links in the chain include the Divine Creator, the angelic heaven, the human, the animal, the world of plants and vegetation, and planet Earth itself with its minerals and waters. In themselves, and in their union together, they proclaim the glory of God (Psalm 104) and the inherent dignity of all things. This image became the basis for calling anything and everything sacred.

What some now call creation spirituality, deep ecology, or holistic gospel actually found a much earlier voice in the spirituality of the ancient Celts, the Rhineland mystics, and, most especially, Saint Francis of Assisi. Women like Hildegard of

Bingen (1098–1179) communicated it through music, art, poetry, and community life itself. Scholars like Saint Bonaventure created an entire *Summa Theologica* based on Saint Francis's spiritual seeing: "In the soul's journey to God we must present to ourselves *the whole material world* as the first mirror through which we may pass over to the Supreme [Artisan]."[58] The Dominican Meister Eckhart (1260–1327) said the same: "If humankind could have known God without the world, God would never have created the world."[59]

The "Catholic synthesis" of the early Middle Ages was exactly that—a synthesis that held together, for us, one coherent world, a positive intellectual vision not defined by being against another or having enemies, but by *the clarity and beauty of form*. It was a cosmic egg of meaning, a vision of Creator and a multitude of creatures that excluded nothing. The Great Chain of Being was the first holistic metaphor for the new seeing offered us by the Incarnation: Jesus as the living icon of integration, "the coincidence of opposites" who "holds all things in unity" within himself (Colossians 1:15–20). God is One. I am whole and so is everything else.

Sadly, we seldom saw the Catholic synthesis move beyond philosophers' books and mystics' prayers. The rest of us Catholics often remained in a fragmented and dualistic world, usually looking for the contaminating element to punish or the unworthy member to expel. While still daring to worship the cosmic Scapegoat—Jesus—we scapegoated the other links in the Great Chain of Being. We have been unwilling to see the Divine Image in those we judge to be inferior or unworthy: sinners, heretics, animals, things growing from Earth, and

Earth itself. Once the Great Chain of Being was broken, we were soon unable to see the Divine Image in our own species, except for folks just like us. Then it was only a short time before the Enlightenment and modern secularism denied the whole heavenly sphere—a denial unknown in any culture except the recent West—and finally the Divinity itself!

As the medievals predicted, once the chain was broken, and one link not honored, the whole vision collapsed. Either we acknowledge that God is in all things or we have lost the basis for seeing God in anything. Once the choice is ours and not God's, it is merely a world of private preferences and prejudices. The cosmic egg is shattered. I am grateful that the positive formulation persisted in the Franciscan motto and coat of arms: *Deus Meus et Omnia* ("My God and All Things").

Saint Bonaventure, who is called the second founder of the Franciscan Order, took Francis's intuitive genius and spelled it out into an entire philosophy. "The magnitude of things . . . clearly manifests . . . the wisdom and goodness of the triune God, who by power, presence and essence exists uncircumscribed in all things."[60] God is "within all things but not enclosed; outside all things, but not excluded; above all things, but not aloof; below all things, but not debased."[61] Bonaventure further expanded on the philosophical idea of God as one "whose center is everywhere and whose circumference is nowhere."[62] Therefore the origin, magnitude, multitude, beauty, fullness, activity, and order of all created things are the very "footprints" and "fingerprints" (*vestigia*) of God. That is quite a lovely and very safe universe in which to live. Welcome home!

Whoever, therefore, is not enlightened by such splendor of created things is blind; whoever is not awakened by such outcries is deaf; whoever does not praise God because of all these effects is dumb; whoever does not discover the First Principle from such clear signs is a fool.

Therefore, open your eyes, alert the ears of your spirit, open your lips and apply your heart so that in all creatures you may see, hear, praise, love and worship, glorify and honor your God, lest the whole world rise against you.[63]

It is hard to imagine how different the last seven hundred years might have been if this truly catholic vision had formed more Christians. Instead, as Bonaventure feared, "The whole world (has now risen in judgment) against" us. Our seeing has been very partial, usually prejudicial, and often not seeing at all. The individual has always decided and discriminated as to where and if God's image would be honored. Sinners, heretics, witches, Muslims, Jews, Indians, native spiritualities, buffalo and elephants, land and water were the losers. Yet we dared to call ourselves monotheists ("one God" tends to move a people toward one world) or "Christ-like." The Divine Indwelling, subject to our whimsical seeing, seems to dwell nowhere except in temples of our choosing. It seems we have always had a "pro-choice movement."

Until we weep over these sins and publicly own our complicity in the destruction of God's creation, we are surely doomed to remain blind. Pope John Paul II reminded us during the Jubilee preparations and in his dramatic pilgrimages of 2000 that this public repentance is necessary. If not, we will likely keep looking for "acceptable" scapegoats. Journalists, politicians, lawyers, and the new restorationists in the church are fervently hunting for sinners these days—in what many claim is a largely secular society. We always think the problem is *elsewhere*, whereas the gospel keeps the pressure of conversion on *us*. As far as the soul is concerned, *no one else is our problem. We are our problem*. "You be converted, and live," says the biblical tradition (see Deuteronomy 30:15–20; Mark 1:15).

Jesus tried desperately to keep us within and connected to the Great Chain of Being by taking away from us the power to scapegoat and project onto enemies and outsiders. We were to keep the chain unbroken by not hating, eliminating, or expelling the other. He commanded us to love the enemy and gave us himself as Cosmic Victim so we would get the point—and stop creating victims—but we are transformed into Christ very slowly.

Our inclination to break the chain—to decide who is good and who is bad—seems to be a basic control mechanism in all of us. We actually are a bit worried about the God in whom Jesus believes: who "causes the sun to rise on the bad as well as the good, who sends down rain to fall on the upright and the wicked alike" (Matthew 5:45). If we dishonor the so-called inferior or unworthy members of creation, we finally destroy ourselves too. Once we stop seeing, we stop seeing. Like nothing else, spiritual transformation is an all-or-nothing proposition. Like Jesus's robe, it is a "seamless garment." He wore it and offers it to us.

Paul did for Jesus exactly what Bonaventure did for Francis.

He took the lived life and made it into a philosophy or theology. The seamless garment is still intact in Paul's most-quoted analogy of the body:

> If one part is hurt, all parts are hurt with it. If one part is given special honor, all parts enjoy it . . . [and] it is precisely the parts of the body that seem to be the weakest which are the indispensable ones, and it is the least honorable parts of the body that we clothe with the greatest care. (1 Corinthians 12:26, 22–23)

Paul, the former mass-murderer Saul, knew well religion's power to create hate and violence toward other people and other links in the Great Chain of Being. He left no room for scapegoating in his teaching: There is "one God and [Creator] of all, over all, through all and within all" (Ephesians 4:6, NJB).

For those given sight by the gospel, there is only one world—God's world—and it is *all* supernatural! We may no longer divide the world into sacred and profane (*fanum* and *profanum*). There is cosmic symbolism in the tearing of the Temple veil from top to bottom at the death of Jesus (Matthew 27:51). In the one world liberated by Christ, our need to divide and discriminate has been denied us—and, frankly, we don't like it. For some reason, we want to retain the right to decide where God is, whom we must honor, and whom we may hate. It's a rather clever guise, for we can remain autonomous and violent while thinking of ourselves as holy. But, as Jesus reminds us, any branch cut off from the vine is useless (John 15:5–6). We either go to God *linked* or it seems we don't go at all.

How easy it is to avoid the sacramental mystery: "Listen, Israel, the Lord your God is One" (Deuteronomy 6:4). Jewish monotheism became the basis for one coherent and cosmic world, where truth is one and there is no basis for rivalry between the arts, science, and religion. If it is true, it is true, regardless of its source. It is such truth that will set us free (John 8:32).

In his brilliant contemporary synthesis, *A Brief History of Everything*,[64] Ken Wilber sounds like a postmodern Thomas Aquinas (1225–1274) or Bonaventure. He concludes that everything is a *holon*. A *holon* is defined as being simultaneously whole within itself and yet also part of something larger. In another book, he explains that everything in the physical, biological, psychic, and spiritual universe is a whole and yet a part.[65] Ours really is *one* connected universe of meaning. In relation to the arrogance of modernism and the cynicism of postmodernism, Wilber notes, "No epoch is finally privileged. We are all tomorrow's food."[66] Agreeing with the genuinely *traditional* Catholic, he reminds us that even our moment in time is a *holon*, a small chain-link in something still larger.

A Great Catholic—one who embraces the whole Tradition—would call this one connected universe the Cosmic Christ, before whom no institution, no moment of time, no attempt at verbalization will be adequate. We must hold the hands of both ancestors and children—and hold them well.

Those who continue to look through microscopes and telescopes are surrendering to the mysteries of an infinite, creative spectrum. The chain of being is even longer and bigger than we church folks imagined—and we had best come to the telescope and microscope with our shoes off, ready to live the emptiness of not knowing. Maybe we are just beginning to see how broad the "communion of saints" might be—and whether we really want to believe in it.

Nine

The Power of Forgiveness

Among the most powerful of human experiences is to give or to receive forgiveness. I am told that two-thirds of the teaching of Jesus is directly or indirectly about this mystery of forgiveness: God's breaking of God's own rules. That's not surprising, because forgiveness is probably the only human action that *reveals three goodnesses simultaneously*! When we forgive, we choose the goodness of the other over their faults, we experience God's goodness flowing through ourselves, and we also experience our own goodness in a way that surprises us. That is an awesome coming together of power, both human and divine.

I want to share a personal story of forgiveness that happened in my family near the time of my mother's death. I was planning to travel home to Kansas, thinking my mother would already be gone by the time I arrived and we'd have the funeral. We had spent many good visits together during her final days and she seemed ready to go. After hearing that she was hanging on, I delayed my arrival for a few days, then took the trip. She was still alive when I arrived and I didn't expect what happened when I got there.

I was sitting by my mother's bed and I told her how I'd miss her. Now, as I have described before, this earthy, farming woman was no sentimentalist. All of a sudden, she said to me, "I want to hear it from him."

I said, "What?"

She said, "Him."

I responded, "You mean Daddy?"

She said, "Yeah, I want to hear if he's going to miss me."

So, I went quickly to my father—at that point, a man of eighty-four, whom we still called "Daddy." For weeks, even months, he had been telling her that he would miss her, but she wanted to hear it one more time from him. So, I said, "Daddy, she wants to hear that you're going to miss her."

He came over and effusively told her, "Oh, I'm gonna miss ya."

She replied, "I don't believe it."

I couldn't believe my ears! I said, "Mother, you're a few hours from death. You can't say that!"

She persisted: "I don't believe it."

Daddy redoubled his efforts: "I ask your forgiveness for all the times I've hurt you in our fifty-four years of marriage and I forgive you for the times you've hurt me."

I said, "Mother, isn't that beautiful? Now, say that back to Daddy."

Suddenly, she closed her eyes and clammed up. She didn't want to say it. (She was a typical Enneagram eight!)

I never felt more the priest. Here, I had to coach my own mother. I said, "Mother, you're soon going to be before God. You don't want to come before God without forgiving everybody."

She said, "I forgive everybody."

I said, "But do you forgive Daddy?" and she became silent again.

Then Daddy jumped in and said, "Honey, I never fooled around with any other women." We all knew that.

She responded, "Well, I know that, I know that."

My siblings and I still don't know what the big issue was, but any married person knows there are many little ways a couple can hurt one another over fifty-four years. There are little grudges, perhaps even big ones, which we hold.

So, I told her, "Mother, you know the Our Father. You're only going to get as much forgiveness from God as you've given. Now, you've got to forgive Daddy."

She kept her eyes closed. I pulled every Christian trick out of the bag, but she kept her eyes closed. Nothing was working.

Then I said, "Mother, let's try this. I'm going to put one hand on your heart and I'm going to pray that your heart gets real soft." I held her other hand and I started kissing it while I held the first hand over her heart.

After about a minute, she said, very faintly, "That melts me."

I responded, "What?"

She said, "When you kiss my hand like that, now I've got to do it."

After a pause, she continued: "I'm a stubborn woman. All my life I've been a stubborn woman."

"Well, Mother, we all knew that," I said. "Now, look at Daddy and you tell him."

So, she looked over—and she didn't say "Daddy," as she usually did. She spoke to him by name: "Rich, I forgive you." (His name was Richard too.)

I prompted her again: "Mother, the other half— 'I ask for your forgiveness.'"

She started breathing really quickly, breathing so heavily I thought it was the end. Then she summoned her energy. She said, "Rich, I ask your forgiveness." She continued with the heavy breathing, then she said, "That's it, that's it. That's what I had to do."

She had been talking for days during the previous week about "a mesh." I couldn't understand what it was. She had said, "There's a mesh that I'm trying to get through."

Now, I said to her, "Mother, do you think that was the mesh?"

She replied, "It's gone! The mesh is gone! And, God, I pray that I mean this forgiveness from my heart."

Then she said, referring to my two sisters and my sisters-in-law, "Tell the girls to do this early and not to wait 'til now. They'll understand a woman's heart and the way a man can hurt a woman."

This took place four days before she died.

Now, this might seem like a tiny thing, but that's the way that we can get clogged up, the way we can be blocked. I'm not sure, but I think all of this might have come from an old quarrel over something most of us would consider insignificant. But, as married people know, some of those struggles carry a deeper symbolic meaning in the relationship.

All we knew was that Daddy occasionally ran over her flowers with the lawnmower. She claimed it was intentional, and we ourselves sometimes wondered. He was the grass man and she was the flower woman, and they both fought for more space. I suppose it was a symbol of something much deeper in their souls—not hard to figure out. On that level, little things can, in fact, be quite deep and significant—symbols, perhaps, but symbolic action is often the real action, especially, it seems, to many women.

Whatever it had been about, I was utterly happy. I said, "Aren't you glad you said it, Mother?"

She responded, "I'm so happy, I'm so happy."

My sister came in a few minutes later and, before I had a chance to tell her the conversation, she talked to mother and then she came running back to me. She said, "Mother says the mesh is gone and she's so happy."

That's the power and the grace of forgiveness—in my own life, with my own stalwart mother.

But let's do it *now* and not wait until later! Let's ask for the grace to let go of those grudges and those hurts to which we cling. How else will we ever be free? Let's live inside of that wonderful good news that says, with Saint Catherine of Genoa, "My deepest me is God!"[67] We have come forth from God, we are sons and daughters, and heirs of something that we did not create. In forgiveness, we live up to our truest dignity. We operate by a power not our own. We live out of the True Self and not just the tiny self that is always offended and complaining. This is the genuinely new thing that true believers have to offer the world.

We Are "Like" God

David Tracy, a powerful American theologian, wrote a book called *The Analogical Imagination*.[68] He concludes that "the great Catholics," who've really been transformed by their catholic worldview, have an "analogical" way of seeing reality. They see God and their own reality as analogous, or "like." It is the result of the Catholic/Christian emphasis on Incarnation, I believe. It always sees heaven and earth as mirroring each other—not distinct, but, in fact, most similar. "As above, so below," we would say—or, if we argue from the other side, "As below, so above." In either case, we have a wonderfully coherent and sacramental universe.

The Catholic mind, at least in its heyday, represented the analogical imagination. It was always emphasizing, "God is like . . . God is similar to. . . . We are the image of. . . . God is the same as . . ." (Saint Bonaventure's *"vestigia Dei,"* the very fingerprints of God). All the world is a poem about God. All of reality is an analogy for God. This, of course, had a good side and a bad side. The good side was that we could be at home in the real world. The *actual* was the place of grace, not the idealized or "religious" world.

We still see this in Mediterranean Catholic countries, where the Catholic imagination took the strongest hold on culture. They don't apologize for fiestas and holidays, for drinking, eating, sex, and dancing. All that was still a bit shadowy to the Nordic Catholics, the Teutonic and Anglo-Saxon types—they never really got the humorous, ironic side of human existence, so well summarized in the poem:

> Wherever the Catholic sun doth shine,
> There's always laughter and good red wine.
> At least I've always found it so.
> *Benedicamus Domino.*[69]

Ironically, this was written by an English Catholic (though of French heritage), Hilaire Belloc (1870–1953).

David Tracy claims that, in general, the Protestant and

Jewish minds imagine things differently. They tend to empha-size *the difference* between God and the world. In the Protestant case, we can see it in the theology of Karl Barth (1886–1968) and many of the Swiss reformers, who continuously emphasize the *otherness* of God. We certainly see that same emphasis on transcendence in much of Jewish spirituality too: "Holy, Holy, Holy, Lord God of Hosts" (Isaiah 6:3). The Incarnation might be unthinkable to most Jews, which is why it is still so strange that it happened amidst the Jewish people! As always, we each have part of the truth. God is both immanent (present in the world) and transcendent (beyond ordinary experience) in good the-ology, it seems to me. We Catholics emphasize the immanence, for good and for ill; Protestants and Jews, and Muslims too, em-phasize transcendence, for good and for ill.

The bad side of reality as an analogy for God was that Catholicism tended to get pretty slack. God was almost too chummy and forgiving. Our Protestant brothers and sisters rightly challenged us on that. At one point, two-thirds of the year was feast days and holidays in Italy. Talk about the oppo-site of the Protestant work ethic! All they did was party! Life meant being at home in this world, with God, one another, and our bodies. The Catholic comfort with drinking is still scandal-ous to many of our Protestant brothers and sisters. But Catholic countries are also notorious for tolerating dictators, political corruption, bribes, greedy upper classes, and non-democratic/non-accountable leadership. Our political record is put to shame by clear-headed Anglo-Saxon and Protestant respect for law and accountability. God as a distant police sergeant does have its social merits.

There has always been a kind of cultural Catholicism which doesn't really take the Gospels seriously (we did not even read them!) or take Jesus's teaching very seriously (we preferred saccharine Sacred Heart novenas). Yet, at the same time, it often produced very compassionate and forgiving people. It retained a kind of mysticism that was lost elsewhere. Protestantism always seemed to produce people who were filled with judgments and criticisms of everything, yet it also produced people much more submitted to the concrete teaching of Jesus and much more socially responsible, in my opinion: the Mennonites on simple living; the Quakers on war; the Lutherans on grace; the Pentecostals on the Holy Spirit; the Amish, Congregationalists, and Presbyterians on different aspects of practical community; the Holiness Churches on sheer joy in God.

At its best, the analogical imagination creates very patient and less judgmental people. I think they feel less judged by God and tend to be more tolerant of others. It's "forgive us as we forgive them" kind of thinking. Perhaps it's nowhere better symbolized in literature than in *The Power and the Glory* by Graham Greene (1904–1991). Greene was a great Catholic in his imaginal world, as were Walker Percy, Victor Hugo, François Mauriac, and Flannery O'Connor. They lived and wrote out of the analogical imagination.

Perhaps you remember the hero of Greene's novel—"the whiskey priest," the drunk! But Greene makes him dear, a saint, an everyman. The shocking idea was that he could still put God on people's tongues. God uses sinners—which is all of us. The whiskey priest was still the mediator between God and humanity, drunk or not. The people still kissed his hand, knowing his sin, but knowing that God forgives all sin, and that we all are sinners. A sincere Protestant could never have written that book. The sinner is too unlike God to ever be used by God or set up as any kind of hero.

If we don't get forgiveness, we're missing the whole mystery. We are still living in a world of meritocracy, of quid-pro-quo thinking, of performance and behavior that earns an award. Forgiveness is the great thawing of all logic, reason, and worthiness. It is a melting into the mystery of God as unearned love, unmerited grace, the humility and powerlessness of a Divine Lover. Forgiveness is the beginning, the middle, and the end of the whole gospel, as far as I can see.

Without radical and rule-breaking forgiveness—received and given—there will be no reconstruction of anything. It alone breaks down our damnable worldview of trying to buy and sell grace. Grace is certainly the one gift that must always be free, perfectly free, in order for it to work. Without forgiveness, there will be no future. We have hurt one another in too many historically documented and remembered ways. The only way out of the present justified hatreds of the world is grace.

What Is Behind Hate?

Hate, though, which I discussed in Chapter Two, is unfortunately here to stay. Hate can be helpful to certain causes. It unites a group quickly, it gives a person identity—even if it is a negative one—and, most of all, it takes away doubt and all free-floating anxiety. It gives us a place to stand that feels superior and in control. Hate settles the dust and ambiguity that none of us likes.

Hate is much more common, and more immediately effective, than love. Hate, as we will sadly see below, makes the world go 'round.

We could say, in fact, that Jesus came to resolve the central and essential problem of hate. There is no other way to save us from ourselves, to save us from one another, and therefore to "save us," unless we are saved from our need to hate. We have produced so much utopian talk about Jesus and love, but Jesus had a very hard time getting to the issue of love. First, he had to expose and destroy the phenomenon of hate. Once he exposed the lie and illusion of hate, love could show itself clearly—and it did.

The pattern is still, unfortunately, the same. As Jesus shockingly put it, "Satan is the real prince of this world" (John 12:31). Hate, it seems, is the ordinary, daily agenda. Love is the totally enlightened, entirely nonsensical way *out* of the ordinary agenda. The gospel presents the dilemma in a personal and cathartic narrative that grounds the whole issue in history and in one man's enlightened response to our history. One man, Jesus, accepts the religious and social judgment of hate and bears the consequences publicly, but in an utterly new way that transforms the pattern and the possibilities. For two thousand years, he has remained the most striking icon of a possible new agenda. His death exposed the lie and the problem like never before. His risen life tells people their lives could have a different story line. He did not just give us textbook answers from a distance, but personally walked through the process and said, "Follow me."

I believe that fear is almost always behind hate. Sometimes it looks like control, but even control freaks are usually afraid of losing something. It is almost always fear that justifies hatred, but a fear that is hardly ever recognized as such. "Even Satan disguises himself as an angel of light" (2 Corinthians 11:14, *NRSV*). The best and most convincing disguise for fear is virtue itself, or godliness. Then it never looks like fear.

For fear to survive, it must look like reason, prudence, common-sense, intelligence, the need for social order, morality, religion, obedience, justice, or even spirituality. It always works. What better way to veil vengeance than to call it justice? What better way to cover greed than to call it responsible stewardship? Only people who have moved beyond ego and the controlling of all outcomes, only those practiced at letting go, see fear for the impostor that it is. To be trapped inside of our small ego is always to be afraid.

To not have anyone that we can trust is necessarily to be a control freak. Thus, great religion tries its best to free individuals from the tyranny of their small and fragile selves. It always points toward a larger identity that we call the Godself, the True Self, the self "hidden with Christ in God" (Colossians 3:3), the trustworthy Lover. Healthy and true religion, like Jesus himself modeled, tells us that there is Someone we *can* trust. We do not have to create all the patterns or fix all the failures. What else would be the beginnings of peace?

If the small ego is not transformed, one other pattern is inevitable. The fear is too destabilizing and unsettling for the small self to bear alone, so it must either be denied or projected elsewhere. The process of both denying *and* projecting our fears and hatreds is called "scapegoating" (as discussed in Chapter Two), from the Jewish ritual of putting our faults on a goat that was whipped out into the desert (see Leviticus 16). The object of our wrath, like the poor "escaping goat," is completely arbitrary and artificial. It has nothing to do with truth or reason. It has to do with fear. With a scapegoat, a plausible and much-needed projection screen will always be found for our little drama.

The amazing thing is how well it works. We rather easily displace our fears onto other people, other issues, other places, and other times. Anything seems better to us than bearing the burden of my-fear-here-now-myself. Only the Great Self can carry such anxiety, such ambiguity, such essential insecurity. It is much too much for the small self to carry.

So, we are stuck with ever new brands of hate. Some have said that the best we have been able to do in the last sixty years is to move hatred to ever-higher forms of sophistication and ever-more subtle forms of disguise. We still love to hate: Feminists can hate men, liberals can hate conservatives, activists can hate rich people, good-family-values folks can hate homosexuals, and victims can hate perpetrators. We just change the vocabulary to make it sound well-considered. This twice-distilled hate is now legitimate, necessary, deserved, and very well disguised! Jesus would call it "driving out the devil by the prince of devils" (see Luke 11:14–23), hating supposed evil and becoming hatred ourselves—but now even more well-hidden from ourselves and difficult to expose. Now we hate under the banner of God, goodness, and political correctness. This is the prince of devils, for sure, a devil almost impossible to drive out.

Paul the Pharisee had to be thrown to the ground and the scales had to painfully fall from his eyes for him to recognize that, in the name of his religion, he had become hate, and even a mass-murderer. The cock had to crow several times before the first pope, Peter, could recognize that he was doing the very thing he said he would *never* do. Yet these are the two figures that stand in front of the largest church in Christendom—as the two pillars of the Roman Church. They were not saints by later, pious definitions. Instead, they were transformed examples of hatred and fear. This is not the rare exception, but the norm and the pattern.

It seems there is something we know by losing and finding that we never would have known by simply being safe and sweet. The greatest lovers are not uncommonly the same people who once hated and feared. Virtue is not just will-power, but actually vice overcome.

Both René Girard and Gil Bailie have taught us that the most effective and common way to turn social hatred into social harmony is via a scapegoat. It works so well, it gathers the community so quickly, that it has endured through most of human history. Now it is the normal story line, so normal that we hardly see it. It remains denied, invisible, and unnoticed.

"Sacred" Violence

C. J. Jung saw the same pattern in the individual that Girard sees in society and culture: That which we fear, deny, and avoid will, with one hundred percent certainty, be projected somewhere else. In other words, there is an intrinsic connection between fear, hatred, and violence. Furthermore, we will do it with impunity and even grandiosity. It is the sacralization of violence and the most common form of violence. That way, we can be hateful and not feel the least bit guilty about it— but, in fact, feel morally superior!

The process of creating sacred violence is so effective that it is now in the "hard wiring" of human personality. As Aquinas noted, no one intentionally does evil. They have to explain it to themselves as good! I am sad to say that, historically, religion is the most effective proponent of hatred and fear, and therefore violence.

Sacred violence is the most common kind of violence. How strange that we could ever arrive at this place after Jesus said that he came for "the forgiveness of sin" (Matthew 26:28) and to share the perfect love that casts out all fear! It's no surprise that he has to spend a great part of his ministry in an effort to reform religion itself. Religion is, ironically, the safest place to hide from God! In its healthy forms, it is also the place to find God. As the Latin saying goes, *corruptio optimi pessima* (the corruption of the best is the worst of all).

We see the classic pattern already in Adam's treatment of Eve and Cain's killing of Abel. It is the original lie and has continued nonstop until now. It is called history: largely a record of who kills, imprisons, tortures, oppresses, controls, enslaves, rapes, occupies, or exploits whom. It's really quite disappointing, once we see it. Then, the utterly predictable response is revenge or retribution. The old and only story line continues unabated. It never stops. At this point, it is getting quite boring. We need a new plot, beyond "get the bad guys."

It is only the mystics and seers in all of the great religions who give us a genuinely new story: redemptive suffering instead of redemptive violence. Socrates, Jesus, the Mother of the Maccabees, Buddha, Harriet Tubman, Gandhi, and Óscar Romero—these give us a genuinely new story line. These few are the true history-makers, who expose the self-serving lie of hatred and open a way through for the rest of us. All others are only delaying the resurrection of humanity.

Resurrection will be taken care of for us, as quietly as a silent Sunday morning, once the lie of "Good" Friday has been exposed and thereby undercut. Once Jesus put all his effort and energy into that Friday, God took care of Sunday easily. But, as the Gospel texts say, "suddenly there was a violent earthquake . . . [and] the guards were . . . like dead men" (Matthew 28:2, 4). The game of smoke and mirrors was over— for good—but there is a continuing seismic shift toward the imperial system.

Love, Infectious and Free

As a Christian, I do believe that Jesus's death was a historical breakthrough, and it is no accident that Christians date history around his life. Afterward, we could never quite see things in the same way. The "virus" of the gospel was forever released into human history, archetypally pictured as blood flowing from the crucified. It was only a minority of Christians who ever got the point, however. Still, the toothpaste cannot be put back into the tube; the movement of grace cannot be reversed.

Most Christians, with utter irony, worshipped Jesus the Scapegoat on Sundays and, on the other six days of the week, made scapegoats of Jews, Muslims, other Christian denominations, heretics, sinners, pagans, the poor, and almost anybody who was not like themselves. One would have thought that Christians who "gazed upon the one they had pierced" (John 19:37) would have gotten the message about how wrong domination, power, and hatred can be. The system had been utterly wrong about their own, chosen God figure, yet they continued to trust the system. I guess they did not gaze long enough.

Many followers of other religions seem to have been infected by the virus more than most nominal Christians. Girard says that the Christian West was the most destabilized by the virus of the gospel, then moved into overdrive to cover its fear and its need to hate, despite the orders from its designated God. The central teaching of Jesus on love of enemies, forgiveness, and care for those at the bottom was supposed to make scapegoating virtually impossible and unthinkable.

Scapegoating depends upon a rather sophisticated, but easily learned, ability to compartmentalize, to separate, to divide the world into the pure and the impure. Anthropologically, all religion begins with the creation of the "impure" and very soon an entire moral system emerges, with taboos, punishments, fears, guilts, and even a priesthood to enforce it. It gives us a sense of order, control, and superiority, which is exactly what the ego wants and the small self demands. But, before you start hating historical religions too much, think about red meat, patriarchy, bourgeois values, all institutions, sexist language, and even Christianity itself. These have become the new "impure" contaminants. (Remember, it only gets more sophisticated and justified!)

The absolute religious genius of Jesus is that he utterly refuses all debt codes, purity codes, religious quarantines, and the searching for sinners. He refuses the very starting point of historic religion. He refuses to divide the world into the pure and the impure, much to the chagrin of almost everybody—then and now.

Jesus is shockingly *not* upset with sinners. This is a shock so total that most Christians, to this day, refuse to see it. He is only upset with people *who do not think* they are sinners: These denying, fearful, and illusory ones are the blockage. They are much more likely to hate and feel no compunction. Formerly, religion thought its mission was to expel sin and evil from River City. Through Jesus, we learn that sin lies in the very act of expelling. There is no place to expel it to. We have met the enemy, and the enemy is *us*. We either carry and transform the evil of human history as our own problem, or we only increase its efficiency and power by hating and punishing it "over there." The Jesus pattern was put precisely and concisely by Paul: "for our sake he made the sinless one a victim for sin, so that in him we might become the uprightness of God" (2 Corinthians 5:21). I admit, that is heavy stuff. Only the mystics and the sinners seem to get it.

In the story of the Good Samaritan, Jesus tells of a man by the side of the road waking up in enemy territory, realizing that he has been loved by the very one who is supposed to hate him and whom he is supposed to fear. Could this be everybody's awakening? Could this be an accurate image of God discovery, and truth discovery? Jesus is clearly presenting the foreign Samaritan as a very image of God. He ends the shocking parable by saying, "Go and do the same" (Luke 10:37). The human task has become the very *imitation of God*, which seems almost unthinkable. God, the one that history has been taught to fear, is in fact the utter Goodness that enfolds us and creates a safe and nonthreatening universe for us—a renewed universe that we can now pass on to others.

For Jesus, there are no postures, group memberships, behaviors, prayer rituals, dietary rules, asceticism, or social awareness that, of themselves, transform us or make us enlightened, saved, or superior. There are no contaminating elements or people to expel or exclude. These will be exposed as inadequate when goodness is exposed all the more. If that is not the moral message that shouts from Calvary, I cannot imagine what the message is.

There is no redemptive violence. There is only redemptive suffering. Yes, hate is the norm, but hate is never the future. It is the old and dead story.

Ten

Limits Are Good Teachers

A wonderful spiritual director from my hometown in Kansas, Loretta Ross-Gotta, once sent me a poem. I would like to begin this chapter with it because it summarizes what I am going to belabor with prose. She called it, "In Praise of Boundaries":

Glory be to God for bounds and limits.

Thanks be for fences, for barbed wire, padlocks, bolts, abrupt unmoving dead ends, for stop signs, ramparts, split rails, outlines, outskirts, contours, confines, borders, margins, hedges and rims, shores, banks and brows.

Blessed art thou for shalts and for shalt nots, for oughts and shoulds, for prohibition, inhibition and command.

I praise thee for enclosure, circumference, courtyard, croft, crib, corral and coupe, pen, balustrade, fold, chamber, hutch and manger, paddock, coat, stall, palisade, parapets, trellis, enclave and wall.

So blessed by thee for bindings, wrappings, swaddling clothes, for all quilts, covers, comforters, and counterpane, for lids, roofs, tents, holes, shell and pod, and all that partitions holy from profane.

Thank you kind and gentle God for edges, parameters, and the delicate beauty of borders, thin, that separate this from that.

Yes from no, the skin from the juice, and thou sweet Trinity from me.

Praise and laud forever unto thee oh thou art a most exulted canopy in thy strong shelter sleeps the virgin safe and free.

All creatures great and small be wary.

As I have discussed earlier in this book, one of the bad effects of the philosophy of progress is that it allowed a group of people to grow up without a sense of appropriate and necessary limits. In the era of supposedly limitless progress, we've expected far too much of one another. Loretta Ross-Gotta's poem, in lauding appropriate limits, names that for me. There must be beginnings and endings to things, it seems. *Only distinct things can, in fact, make love and create union. True union, ironically, differentiates things more than melding them into one.* That is a major and often-confused paradox.

I grew up in the 1960s, reading wonderful books like Josef Goldbrunner's *Holiness Is Wholeness*. I totally agree with that title on one level, but the trouble is that we grew up really expecting things to be whole! What a recipe for disillusionment. We grew up expecting far too much from institutions, from the church, from one another, and, finally, too much from ourselves. We expected the small self to attain the grandeur of God.

Now we have a widespread complaint from young people that they hate themselves. If we really believe that the small self can be whole or if we try to build our self-image on other people's responses, we are set up for disaster. The most we will gain is momentary rushes of significance, episodic self-esteem that will last a couple of days. But it cannot be sustained, except by "upping the dosage," which finally becomes the addictive and destructive personality. Conversely, we will live beneath everyone else's judgments and critiques. It is no surprise that the word *codependent* emerged so strongly in recent decades. Secular people have no other place to live except in a revolving hall of mirrors—which themselves are being mirrored by other mirrors. That's scary. It has created a very fragile kind of person.

Self-esteem comes naturally when I am aligned with who-I-am-in-God. It is inherently unstable when I try to create it out of my own psyche, behavior, or fame. The small self on its own, or seeking its significance through the approval of others, will never finally ground us, because the next day we have to say again: "What do I do today to be important, to be significant, to be well-regarded? How can I be famous for more than twenty minutes? Maybe my only choice is infamy?" Often, when the positive cannot be attained or sustained, people move toward the negative for cosmic significance: "At least I can get my name in the paper for killing everybody at school or shooting a famous person."

The false self, the small self, the autonomous I, "the branch cut off from the Vine is useless" (John 15:4–5). We had the right idea about being *whole*, but the trouble is that we thought we could do it independently and within our private personality. That is the eternal lie of the ego. The ego refuses to admit its own limits and boundaries, and thus always self-destructs. It either inflates itself by itself (pride), or it deflates under the awareness of its own insufficiency (self-hatred).

Entitlement Is a Poor Teacher

A sense of limits offers a much more honest attitude about what we can expect from life. We are set up for anger and judgment when we expect too much from one another, from the world, and from institutions. This is a sense of entitlement, and characterizes most people who are rich, from developed countries, and most younger people born into the new world of "rights." Our parents and grandparents grew up instead in a world of responsibility. We are still searching for the happy middle between those two.

Most people in developing countries learn a sense of limits much earlier. Observing such people is what gives me the courage to speak this way. People in developing countries are usually in need and have a right to more, to justice, but they also have *a much more honest expectation of reality*. They have a more properly shaped ego. The tragic, the broken, and the sinful are already woven into reality. We in the West have gotten away with a false entitlement that did not weave the tragic into our worldview. We actually suffer more because of it. Anyone who has been there will tell you that the poor in developing countries tend to smile more than the middle class or the wealthy in any country.

Remember, the cross tells us that there is *a cruciform pattern to all reality*, a collision of cross-purposes, as discussed in Chapter Two. Our world is filled with contradictions needing to be reconciled, inconsistencies within us and between us. Life is neither perfectly consistent and rational nor is it a chaotic mess. It does contain, however, constant paradoxes, exceptions, and flaws. That is the shocking and disappointing revelation of the cross. It is also a great weight off our backs. It leads to patience, humility, nonjudgment, and suffering love. Now we have the right sense of proportion, limits, and expectations, with no room for utopianism, ideologies, any "final solutions," cynicism, or needless discouragement. The shape of things is finally honest and humble. Here we can live with *faith* (that God is in the contradictions) instead of grandiose explanations. Please think about that at great length!

People are talking about this when they talk about simple living. Simplicity of lifestyle might be, after all, the most radical form of social justice possible. It is a non-pretentious way of simply living outside of the whole system of greed, consumption, and injustice. Simplicity will clearly have to be part of any kind of reconstruction. Any rebuilding must move toward a more modest sense of self. The grandiose self is like a fragile but giant balloon, bouncing around a room and often demanding more inflation to avoid the inevitable. In the postmodern world, people set themselves up to be offended and to be addictive by their false sense of entitlement. Yet, the only real entitlement is from God. When our "name is written in heaven" (Luke 10:20), then all other titles are superfluous and even burdensome.

Ken Keyes (1921–1995) wrote, "You add suffering to the world just as much when you *take* offense as when you *give* offense."[70] We've created a highly offendable people who think they deserve an awful lot— and even have a right to it. The small self has to puff itself up because underneath it knows it is all a sham. A friend of mine who is an airline attendant said that attendants often fight over who has to take the first-class section of the plane. No one wants it, she said. The people are much more fun and more appreciative in economy class.

Entitlement is a big theme in Alcoholics Anonymous. Many with addictive personalities have lost so much that they feel the world owes them. It is a form of narcissism, but it goes beyond the addictive personality. Such narcissism has led America to become a highly litigious society, where we sue other people when they do not give us what we think we have earned or have a right to. I am told that America has seven times as many lawyers as Japan, and many more than most other countries. We go to the level of court, law, and money to achieve what the court, law, and money will never be able to give us: self-esteem. Only God can give us our dignity. Maybe that is why Paul told the early Christians never to go to court (1 Corinthians 6:7–8).

The True Self Has Never Been Hurt

The True Self can never be hurt, nor has it ever been hurt. The only pain it suffers is longing for God and absence from God. It is only the false self that suffers and takes offense. Hopefully those sufferings lead us to collapse back into the True Self. The false self is necessarily insecure and always hurt.

The True Self is indestructible and cannot be offended. The True Self does not stand around waiting for us to like it before it can like itself. It doesn't wait for accolades or external successes before it can believe in itself. It quietly knows.

G. K. Chesterton spoke of the "mystical minimum," which he defined as *gratitude*.[71] When we stand in the immense abundance of the True Self, there is no time or space for being hurt. We are always secure, at rest, and foundationally grateful.

The grateful response for what is given—seeing the cup half full—requires seeing with a completely different set of eyes than the eyes that always see the cup as half empty. I don't think it's an oversimplification to say that people basically live either in an overall attitude of gratitude or an overall attitude of resentment. The mystical minimum is gratitude: Everything that is given—that we are breathing today—is pure gift. None of us has earned it. None of us has a right to it. All we can do is kneel and kiss the ground—somewhere, anywhere, everywhere.

I certainly believe in human rights and would not want to make light of them, but the Bible never talks about human rights as such. The only rights the Bible talks about are the rights of widows, orphans, and the poor. The little ones have rights that must be respected, and the Word of God always protects the bottom-dwellers and the unprotected. But, in our typical Western narcissism, we use God to protect the top, the elite, those who have too much already. Welfare used to be for the unemployed; now it is for auto manufacturers and the military! Even the Canon Law of the Church protects the clergy's rights much more than those of the laity or of the widows and orphans. I well remember the excellent poster that stated: "It will be a great day when our schools get all the money they need and the Air Force has to hold a bake sale to buy a bomber."[72]

We wait, it seems, for a shift in consciousness from an exclusive sense of rights and entitlement to consciousness balanced with a sense of responsibility and social obligation. We seem still to be on one side of that swing of the pendulum. When civilization is growing and empowering, it makes use of the language of responsibility: what we, in fact, *owe* to our family, our people, our country, the earth, God. The present ungrateful complaining and blaming will get us nowhere. Now we can play the victim and use justice language, or falsely claim, "I am suing only because I don't want this to happen to others"—for our own advantage. In fact, this can be the most disguised power trip of all, and just the opposite of how Jesus used his victimhood. He used it to liberate others. We use it to empower ourselves and to punish others.

We do have rights, and most of us thank God for this new insistence on human rights and human dignity, but someone must also protect the rights of the *whole*, the common good. If people do so today, they are considered moralistic, dogmatic, or coercive. Here, the conservatives are far ahead of most "progressive" thinkers, who have made an idol of individuality and personal freedom or license. Someone does have the right to protect society, institutions, and groups. If all we have is individual rights, we will tear one another apart in the fray.

I think we have created a mentality that disallows any *calling power* over us. We want to live as if no one is ever going to tell us what we need to do, as if we are the final arbiters of all our decisions, all our choices. We will not allow other persons or institutions—not even our marriage partner in some cases—to make demands on us. Free choice itself has become our idol. "I choose, therefore I am" has become the new Cartesian formula. I am afraid such "freedom" will end up destroying all freedom for everybody. The only way to hold such a society together will be by more and more laws, and enforcement of those laws. Then there are the endless prisons to hold those who do not comply, after we idealize "free choice" for them! Restraint and limits are declared unvirtuous in our society—except that the poor and the criminally inclined are supposed to practice them! I do not think we can have it both ways.

Virtue is not one isolated value, but a relationship between several values. When personal freedom is isolated from love, temperance, and the common good, we have a demon instead of a virtue. True virtue is another name for Sophia or Holy Wisdom. Wisdom is clearly more than mere intelligence, knowledge of facts, or information. Virtuous people recognize limits, balance, and other people's virtues too. Wisdom is more synthesis than analysis, more paradoxical than linear, more a dance than a march. Wise people avoid the ideological hysteria that claims, "This is the whole truth, the only truth, the only way to look at it," too often in the name of some denied but self-serving concern.

When we have a new insight or experience, we tend to absolutize that experience and dismiss everything prior to it. I see a lot of that in America since we are a "now" society. We read a new book and temporarily see what we find there as the only way to interpret everything— throwing out the first thirty years of our lives and all other paradigms of explanation. No wonder people are fragmented.

We can usually mistrust any explanation that says "only." At that point, we are dealing with idealized, fabricated realities (false religion) and not incarnate and cruciform reality (true religion). It is precisely in this sense that *Christianity is true religion*. Christianity teaches us a *process* of humility, waiting, ego surrender, patience, and trust, much more than merely giving us prefabricated *content* to defend or prove. Some Hindus and Buddhists have this true religion much more than many Christians. Many of us prefer only ways of thinking over a process of transformation, which always asks us to "die."

Erasmus the Reconstructionist

At the very end of the medieval era, as the Reformation was challenging all the old paradigms with new ways of thinking and relating, Erasmus of Rotterdam (1466–1536) charted a course of reconstruction. Perhaps you've heard of him. There probably would have been no painful dividing of Europe over the Reformation if the people had heard Erasmus instead of aligning with either the pope on one side or Martin Luther on the other. Dualistic thinking won—and therefore we all lost. Either/or thinking never leaves room for the wonderful *third* something. Erasmus was a third-something person.

Erasmus stood patiently in the middle and said that there was truth in both what the pope and Luther were saying. (Only four hundred and fifty years later, in 1999, did the Catholics and Lutherans agree that they had been saying the same thing!) But Erasmus, by and large, was unheeded. He calmly kept speaking, trying to persuade each to see the other's side, but both were trapped in their own ideological hysteria—the same pattern we see in so many places and groups today. The divided mind led to a divided and warring Europe, and Christian divisions that last to this day.

Erasmus stressed actions over formal theology. He held that there should be an absolute minimum of theology. In that, we see a similarity with the reconstructive approach of Saint Francis. True spirituality doesn't require much middle management. Basically, we have to teach people how to see and then they'll see for themselves. Of course, teaching people how to see isn't easy, because we also have to teach them to see *all the way through* and to see *everything*. It's major surgery to get that ego and those private agendas out of the way so we can see. Erasmus emphasized epistemology over metaphysics, *how* we see over *what* we see.

The best ally of God is reality—not theology, not ideology, not what *should be* as much as what *is*. Erasmus said that no Christian—especially no child—needs or is capable of digesting the thoroughgoing encyclopedic catechism that gives an answer for every conceivable question that we could possibly run into—and the answer, in fact, makes the journey unnecessary.

Erasmus felt it was precisely that mindset that had gotten the Church in trouble for much of its fifteen-hundred-year history, and then Luther too, thinking the catechism could and should explain everything. Erasmus questioned, "Is it not possible to have fellowship with the Father, Son and Holy Spirit, without being able to explain philosophically the distinction between them?"[73] He was saying then what liberation theologians would say in the late twentieth century, that Jesus clearly taught orthopraxy (right behavior) much more than orthodoxy (right ideas).

I think the church must come to respect the limits of human understanding and of its own understanding of mystery. Strangely, it teaches the first but denies the second. The institutional church has to get beyond needing answers and theological conclusions for every possible scenario that arises—yet we are the very ones who love to preserve the notion of mystery! I do not think we can have it both ways. We should be the protectors of mystery, not the explainers of it. Probably it's a natural outgrowth of the Greco-Roman model of organization that influenced us so much. The Eastern Church seems much more comfortable with mystery.

Cynics are often those who once expected too much. When we put all our eggs in one basket—expecting everything from this institution—we're setting ourselves up for major disappointment. I think that's behind a lot of the disillusionment that so many Catholics have gone through in recent years. Yes, we need to take the institution seriously—just about as seriously as Jesus took the institution of Judaism. My point is that we shouldn't take it overly seriously. Jesus radically critiqued Judaism. As in the rest of life, we need to say "yes" to something before we're free to say "no," but we must also say "no" when needed, or we have idolatry, the major sin of the Hebrew Scriptures.

The Case of the Birth Control Encyclical

Let me give you a difficult, unpopular example. One of the encyclicals (papal teachings) that has probably been most criticized is Pope Paul VI's 1968 encyclical, *Humanae Vitae* (*On Human Life*). The media, and most of the Catholic Church, picked up on its prohibition of artificial birth control and missed all the rest.

Many of its critics haven't read it. *Humanae Vitae*'s theology is excellent, but liberals assume it has nothing to say and conservatives bow down in front of it before they have read it. This is not the wonderful third something because it leaves us all in our split minds.

In fact, most of the sense of limits, goals, and values in the encyclical are really excellent. I would bet that ninety-five percent of the readers of this book would say the same thing if they actually read it. But we seem never to get beyond either a Western mistrust of authority or an ideological bias toward all authority. Authority and truth are really not the same principle. *Jesus came to give us a truth that would set us free, not an authority that would do all our homework for us.* Institutional religion is doing God no favor by setting up a professional teaching station, which itself becomes the issue instead of the gospel values themselves. We either love this teaching station or we hate it, and never get to "justice, mercy, and good faith" (Matthew 23:23).

Instead of being thinking and faithful people, we live, like our culture as a whole, with sound bites and one-liners. We either react against the whole thing uncritically or buy the whole thing uncritically—instead of saying, "What are the values here that are worth hearing? What are the truths here about marital love, faithful love, about communication and relationship?" That's the big point of *Humanae Vitae*, by the way: communication between husband and wife, mutual respect, mutuality. This is the same agenda that the feminists are rightly seeking.

For us as Christians, the highest value should *always* be love. If we're going to accept the Judeo-Christian heritage as meaningful and authoritative in any way, we have to admit that love comes first and last. That puts us on a different track and forces a different set of questions. The deepest questions are not those of rights and power, or whether or not we're getting everything that society owes us. The deepest questions are those of how love can be expanded and increased. How can we "defer to one another out of reverence for Christ" (Ephesians 5:21)?

This is a third way, a new something wonderful. The dualistic and merely political mind will never understand it. It reads everything in terms of win/lose, right/wrong, good/bad, either/or, top/bottom. Only the contemplative mind, the new consciousness made possible by God-experience and prayer, can read reality in a panoramic and truly wisdom fashion (see 1 Corinthians 2:12–16 in this regard). The calculating mind, the egocentric vision, is all that the system has. We have a new mind, made possible by God.

Eleven

Living with Shadow

Spiritual transformation is often thought of as movement from darkness to light. In one sense that is true, but, in another sense, it is totally false. We forget that darkness is always present alongside the light. Pure light blinds. Only the mixture of darkness and light allows us to see. Shadows are required for our seeing. God alone lives in perfect light (James 1:17).

In a certain sense, we know the light most fully in contrast with its opposite. Christian theology has traditionally talked about the "happy fault," the idea that if Christ had not been crucified, he would not have experienced the Resurrection. Again, there is something we can only know by going through the "night-sea journey"[74] into the belly of the whale, from which we are spit up on an utterly new shore.

Western civilization has failed to learn how to carry the shadow side. We did not evangelize through our living icon, Jesus. Instead, we developed a system involving winners and losers, which is not Jesus. Because we did not teach our people how to carry the paschal mystery, it is now coming back to haunt us. Catholics have no ability to carry the shadow side of the church, nor the shadow side of the papacy, nor the shadow side of the clergy. It is always all-good or all-bad, never *both crucified and resurrected at the same time*, as Christ is. Catholic politics is not known worldwide for creating negotiators, mediators, compromise, or peacemaking. Let's be humble enough to admit it, and weep over our sins. In that sense, we are not the hope of the world!

In many ways, it's been a constant dilemma of the church. It wants to live in perfect light, where God alone lives. It does not like the shadowland called earth, its only home. We see in Christian history the Eastern Church trying to create heavenly liturgies with little sense of social justice, Luther's abhorrence of his own shadow, the Swiss Reformers trying to outlaw darkness, the Puritans trying to repress shadow, the Roman Church consistently unable and unwilling to see its own shadow, the typical believer afraid of their shadow, and the new fundamentalists preoccupied with Satan. Then comes the postmodern world, in predictable pendulum swing, in love with shadows! All of us, it seems, are trying to find ways to avoid the mystery in human life, instead of learning how to carry it patiently, as our humble Jesus did.

There are no perfect structures and there are no perfect people. There is only the struggle to get there. It is Christ's passion (*patior*, the "suffering of reality") that will save the world. "Your patient endurance will win you your lives," says Luke (21:19). Redemptive suffering instead of redemptive violence is the Jesus way. Patience comes from our attempts to hold together an always-mixed reality, not from expecting or demanding a perfect reality. That only makes us resentful and judgmental, which is what has characterized much of Christian history. I agree with those who have said they don't like religious people very much. Who likes people who can never deal patiently with limits and shadow, which is just about everything?

One reason Nietzsche evidently did not trust Christians was because they seemed to be filled with resentment. False expectations create resentful people, like Sisyphus, rolling the stone up the hill and knowing it will roll back down. Grateful people emerge in a world rightly defined, where even the shadows are no surprise, but, in fact, opportunity.

Our failure to carry the shadows as individuals has moved to a secular level too. We refuse to carry the shadow side of institutions, groups, nations, or periods of history. We look for races and nations to blame instead of admitting that we are all in this human thing together. Every culture, in my opinion, is a mixture of shadows and light.

There is not much point in deciding the exact percentages, or, like children, fighting over who hit whom first. Go back far enough and we all oppressed others or were oppressed ourselves. In the big picture, there is no moral high ground on which to stand. Whoever has the power, oppresses. That is normative, and it includes native peoples, Jews, blacks, and women. When they are on top, they do the same thing. Jesus reframed the question around power, not ethnicity, religion, or gender. He stepped out of the whole cycle by riding into Jerusalem on a donkey, outside the symbols of power.

Maybe we avoid shadows because they are an in-depth experience of our own powerlessness and poverty. None of us wants to be a part of any imperfect group or institution. Perhaps because we did not resolve the question on a personal level, we have no ability to deal with it on a historical level. We keep looking for some perfect pedestal on which to stand, some place where we can be clean, pure, and above it all. Remember, the very notion of religion begins with the creating of the concept of impurity. Jesus ended religion, as we know it, forever.

Learning in the Shadows

Shadowlands are good and necessary teachers. They are not to be avoided, denied, fled, or explained away. They are not even to be forgiven too quickly. First, like Ezekiel the prophet, we must eat the scroll that is "lamentation, wailing, and moaning" in our belly, and only eventually sweet as honey (see Ezekiel 2:9–3:3). When we're in the shadows, there's a loss of meaning and motivation. By the time most people reach middle age, they have experienced days when they just can't find life—joy isn't there. We call it depression, and some form of it happens to most people at some time. In its extreme form, it requires medical attention, but clinical depression is not what we're talking about here (although it could take that form if we do not find God in it).

There's a shadowland where we are led by our own stupidity, our own sin, our own selfishness, by living out of the false self. We have to work our way back out of this with brutal honesty, confessions and surrenders, some forgiveness, and often by some necessary restitution or apology. The old language would have called it repentance, penance, or stripping. By any account, it is major surgery and feels like dying (although it also feels like immense liberation). We need help at these times. Alcoholics Anonymous seems to be very good in its advice at this stage, even for non-alcoholics.

There's another shadowland, however, into which we're led by God and grace, and the nature of the journey itself. In many ways, the loss of meaning here is even greater, and sometimes the loss of motivation is greater. The loss of purpose, boundaries, and directions might be greater too. It really feels like the total absence of light, and thus the saints called it "the dark night." But the difference is that we still sense that we have been led here intentionally, somehow. We know we are in liminal space, betwixt and between, on the threshold—and we have to stay here until we have learned something essential. It is still no fun—filled with doubt and "demons" of every sort—but it is the dark night of God. All transformation takes place in such liminal space.

The dark night into which we lead ourselves by sin can also become the shadowland of God. Maybe this is even the most common pattern. But there is nevertheless a "good" shadowland and a "bad" shadowland, basically having to do with whether we see God in it. The wound can become the sacred wound, or it can just remain a bleeding, useless wound with a scab that never heals. *Salvation is, most commonly, sin overcome in the biblical tradition, not just sin avoided.* It's the sin that becomes salvation, but it's the same event, the same experience.

In shadowed times, there's usually an overwhelming sense of not belonging, of not fitting in. There are days when we feel nothing will console us and the old things that we used to do no longer work. There's no friend to call who could take this pain away. That's when, of course, we're driven to prayer. We either find God then, or go into a deep freeze.

Normally, there's a reluctance to talk to helpful people, or to the people we once trusted. This feels like an act of rebellion against any kind of help. We close down. Many of my generation said proudly, "Don't trust anybody over thirty!" We had seen our father figures almost totally sell out to militarism and materialism. We could not trust them as mentors of spirituality or wisdom. We hated their shadows and then fell into our own. Unfortunately, we seem now to be experiencing a universal non-trust, a universal rebellion. Why should I trust any politician or priest or president? They've shown that they are not good leaders. We are, of course, half right. But there is another half.

We're often rebelling against our own inner priesthood, our own inner prophet who might know the way for us. We're actually *choosing* to sit in the shadows, and maybe that is necessary too. Normally, in the shadows, there's restlessness, a type of inner pacing. It's almost as if going backward and forward on the same path is an image of who we are—not really wanting to go in any direction, just turning around as if we're going to find the answer in between. Maybe we need this deconstruction before we can rightly reconstruct on the foundations of the True Self.

In that restlessness, we not only can't pray, we don't want to pray. Of course, then we are throwing out the only inner authority we might have, or the only wisdom we might trust. We don't even want to trust God. We don't want to pray because God might have an answer, and then we would have to act. We don't want to act. The tragic, the paralysis, the self-pity all have a strange attraction.

When we have reached this point, we usually start looking for someone to blame. The stupidity of blaming is that it absolves us from solving the problem within ourselves. Blaming will not do the soul work. It will not remain with the paradox. It splits instead, releasing the *eustress* (good stress), the creative anxiety. Yet, staying with the paradox, the *eustress*, refusing to compartmentalize the good and the bad, might be the most courageous thing we have ever done.

To stay with the paradox is an immense act of courage, and why some moralists have said courage is the foundational virtue. The word courage comes from *cor-agere*, "an act of the heart," which we now know has its own kind of intelligence.[75] Now we know that all our poetry and music about the heart was not just poetry and music, but correct intuition.

While experiencing a sense of loss of meaning, it is very difficult to try to self-generate courage; we can only draw it from others. We look for signs around us that maybe life has meaning for someone else. We wait for positive contagion. Sometimes we just look for a smile. I've experienced that in little ways, from simple kindnesses of store clerks or from small exchanges at the kiss of peace during Mass. I may have been just going through the motions of Mass, and then, at the kiss of peace, some loving, good person looks into my eyes and really seems to mean it and say it, and I come back to the altar transformed.

What it comes down to, so often, is the power of simple love to lead us out of meaninglessness. It sounds so naïve and so simplistic, but love is still the greatest healer, the great transformer, and the greatest giver of meaning. Love aligns us. Yet, during shadow times, love is the very thing we resist and almost make impossible. "I will prove that I am unworthy. I will not let you get to me." There is an almost demonic energy at that point. That is the real absence of light in these periods. We can see no way out from within.

Good Doubt

In the shadows, we doubt everything. For most people, deep change starts with doubt about day-to-day things. Then they move into mental doubts, then ethical doubt about who is right and who is wrong. Finally, they move into absolute doubt or total cynicism. To change fundamentally, we have to go all the way to the bottom. When we're at the point of absolute doubt, then we—hopefully—look for new meanings (although some people remain there and make skepticism a way of life). There are many signs that some aspects of our culture today are fixed in a state of absolute doubt. It is only good to pass through times of doubt, not to stay there.

Out of the chaos often comes the greatest creativity. The only thing that can endure deep doubt is faith. We will not allow ourselves to go into the deeper levels of doubting without, in fact, a very strong faith. That's the opposite of what most people think. I fault the tradition here, for telling us that doubt was a bad thing. Those who can endure great doubt, in my experience, have been those who rise to great faith. Faith gets purified every time we go through the cycle of doubt and failure, saying, "Why do I believe this? Do I believe this at all? On what do I base my life?" On this wheel of fortune, just about everything is purified: self-image, God-image, worldview.

If there were compassion and forgiveness in someone's early models of authority, then there will undoubtedly be a readiness to believe in a God of compassion and forgiveness. So, of course, people who have been surrounded by compassion and love have a great big head-start on the true image of God and reality in general.

It takes a long time to purify the experience of dysfunctional family life, abuse, manipulation, shaming, negative attitudes toward anything, totalitarian attitudes, or judgmental attitudes. They're only purified in desperate situations where the old god doesn't work anymore, the old self and old attitudes don't work anymore. As Saint John of the Cross described, our gods must each die until we find the true God. As Meister Eckhart put it, "I pray God to rid me of God."[76] Each dying god is another shadow and another death, which is probably why the great mystics speak of dark nights so much.

Cultural Shadows and Crisis

I think we've been led into a period of exile again, both as a culture and as a church. In the periods of shadow, we feel a lot of hostility. We take it out on other people by blaming them. Often, all it takes to stem this process is for one person to take a hopeful stance. One time, I was sitting with a family who had just come back from Sunday morning Mass. They were pretty much damning the morning Mass and the priest—I guess it wasn't a very good liturgy or homily. The father of the family calmly brought another perspective. He said, "Listen, I have my bad days. Can't we give him credit? He had a bad day today." Suddenly, the whole tone changed, through the quiet leadership of a father of a family. Imagine how dead-ended and useless it would have been if he simply joined in on the crucifying. I am not saying there is no place for criticism, but there is the kind that opens possibility and the kind that merely spews and increases negative energy.

There's a lot of freedom in being able to say something like that father did, in a crowd going in the opposite direction. It takes spaciousness inside to give spaciousness to others. In this case, he gave space for both the priest and for his family to grow. Maybe spaciousness is a good definition of compassion. It is certainly a good description of a third way.

The temptation in shadow times is to pull back from others, to move into a self-chosen exile. Then evil festers, because evil festers when people are cut off, which happens to be my criticism of so much of the prison system. Whenever we separate people in a state of alienation, evil festers; it doesn't decrease. It's the same when we pull into our personal prisons, our chosen exiles. That's when marriages end, when there's a refusal to remain in the dialogue. The very word *diabolical* means to throw apart. Thus we have the insidious nature of modern individualism. We cannot retreat there, although it is a great temptation in confused times such as these.

Much pulling back is not out of discernment—so that we can hear better, like the desert retreats of Jesus. More frequently, we pull back out of fear, and sometimes out of contempt for others, or perhaps for the church because it has not served us well. I wonder if some people's rejections are not an extended form of their own self-loathing. No one is more anti-Catholic than Catholics, it seems. No one bemoans, betrays, and tears down their own tradition more than Christians. People who hate themselves hate others just like them.

When spiritual issues are not resolved in our own lives, when compassion is not found in our immediate sphere, we hate the groups, the history, and the ancestry of which we're a part. We overreact against it. Here again is the refusal to carry the shadow side—this time the shadow side of our own tradition. Those of us who are Catholic have a long tradition to carry: two thousand years of silliness—and two thousand years of saints.

We are formed both by "the right hand of God" and "the left hand of God." The right hand of God is always the gratuity, the wonder, the loveliness of life. The left hand of God is always the painful mystery of things, and the left hand of God is just as essential in our formation as the right hand of God. It is the *whomp* on the side of the head that gets our necessary attention. Then we can hear and receive something new and good.

The way through is always much more difficult than the way around. Cheap religion gives us the way around. True religion gives us the way through. Cheap religion denies the shadows. True religion steps right into them.

The Traps Inside

When we're in the shame-and-blame game, which is when we're in the shadows, we'll usually be masters of projection. We know that our hatred of others is normally a projection of our own inner state. That's why Jesus taught that, for the sake of *our* soul, we *must* love the enemy. The enemy carries our shadow side. Look carefully for those you resent, because they're normally carrying at least some of what you hate or deny or reject within yourself. Again, Jesus said it first: "Why do you try to take the speck out of your brother or sister's eye, when you cannot see the log in your own?" (Matthew 7:4). Normally, it is here, in us, before it is there.

We let our feelings out against the group or against the

community instead of realizing that this is a time when God can teach us. We must think: "Perhaps this is a lesson. How can I learn from this too?" Normally, at that point, we do need a spiritual friend; it's almost impossible to pull ourselves out of the pit alone. Someone else has to "preach the gospel" to us. I know, as a preacher, that I usually cannot preach to myself.

We also need a guide because we're in uncharted territory. We don't know how to get out of the shadows, so it's easier to just sit there and justify being there. We tend to seek out friends who give us the justification for being there, who keep bemoaning the terrible situation and legitimating our hurts. It's Job, sitting on the dung heap, and his stupid friends giving him further reasons for staying there. Remember how he picked at his sores with a potsherd (Job 2:8)? We keep replaying the old tapes and re-biting ("re-morse") the old, sour food. Just like Job, we sit on our dung heap for seven days and seven nights (2:13).

The temptation of our group, our family, our community is to be threatened by our negativity. They don't want to hear it, perhaps because they might be drawn in by the truth that's there. Some fear all critical thinking because they fear that the structures will collapse. I see this in so many of the neoconservatives who cannot tolerate any criticism of the church, or the patriots and flag-worshipers of America.

There is such a thing as healthy criticism. People who love something have also earned the right to make it better and keep it true to its deepest vision. All criticism is not blind negativity; it can also carry hope and vision when we own the problem. When we recognize that we are an accomplice in the evil and also complicit in the good, and take responsibility for both, when we can use the language of "us" and not "them," then we are bearing the full mystery of something. Then our criticism is coming from love, not hate.

Two Sides of Truth

In general, the only people I really trust to do reconstruction work are people who have paid their dues to deconstruction. If someone has never been able to see the shadow side, they haven't gained the right to talk the language of reconstruction. We need to have seen the shadow side, have felt the sour stomach, and have emerged renewed from the belly of the whale. We don't need naïve people or people in denial. We need people who have been there, know the problems, and have come out alive.

We need to have pulled away from the idolatry of the system in order to gain the authority and the credibility to walk back in and work for reconstruction.

If all we can do is criticize and negatively point out the shadow side, however, we have another set of problems. There's no gift of hope or positive energy here; there is only paralysis. An insecure community or group cannot tolerate criticism. As I said earlier, it was a sign of the maturity of the Roman Catholic Church that it could self-criticize during the Second Vatican Council in the 1960s. A healthy family can—in fact, must—own its dirty laundry. As the alcoholics say, "we are as sick as our secrets." We are also as healthy as the way we criticize.

Whatever you say about the 1960s, that movement began the current deconstruction in earnest. It was a healthy period of self-criticism of culture and church. How different it was from the idolatry of the 1980s, when both pope and president (Reagan) could no longer allow criticism! The Catholic Church was again the only way to go to heaven and America was the promised land. It is especially strange that the Roman Catholic Church, which insists that sins cannot be forgiven without naming them in confession according to kind, number, and intention, has been unable to do the same. Thank God, Pope John Paul II began to correct this long pattern of corporate pride and non-repentance in his public confessions of Lent 2000. Unfortunately, the last American president (Trump) has reverted to disallowing any type of American self-criticism.

The shadowlands are sacred ground. Our trust is that the God who has called us into this present moment will also sustain us and lead us through it. Undoubtedly, we're in a shadowy, potentially transformative period. In a certain sense, there is only one definition of the biblical God. YHWH and Jesus are always the ones "who bring the dead to life and call into being what does not yet exist" (see both Deuteronomy 32:39 and Romans 4:17). It is the one and only pattern of God, and we must be ready for it, again and always.

While material goods decrease as we make use of them, spiritual goods increase as we use them. We are ready to make use of our immense spiritual power. What is genuinely exciting is that many of these gospel gifts are being discovered and used outside the explicitly defined community of faith—since we seem to have neglected them. I don't suppose God cares which group gets the credit. It is all God's work anyway. When *A Course in Miracles* (a self-study course in spiritual psychology), Alcoholics Anonymous, along with prison reform systems, social workers, and ecologists make use of spiritual power, it will only increase and spread. Maybe Jesus was speaking of his own community when he warned against burying the gift out of fear (see Matthew 25:24–25) instead of using it with abandon.

The religious worldview is essentially hope-filled. Any experience of grace tells us that history is not about us. In fact, my own life is not about me! History is more than human history; it's also God's history, the planet's history, the history of the life and death of God in all things. Who would not want to be a part of that? Sometimes I find archeologists, nurses, marine biologists, and Hindu mothers of six who enter trustfully into this great mystery more than those of us who have been officially baptized into it. They are useable for God.

Toppling the Idols

As we get closer to the real thing, opposition will rise, just as it rose around Jesus. It's very scary whenever we're moving to a new synthesis or paradigm, especially for those who are heavily invested in the old. They usually have much to lose. They don't necessarily have ill will; it's just that they're living in the only world they've ever imagined.

Human beings tend to live inside of our small comfort zones. We put all our trust and security in institutions, jobs, explanations, even in sacred things like family. It's no surprise that Jesus has to call the first disciples away, not from *bad* things, but from good things like family and job (see Mark 1:19–20).

People will feel we are being negative or violent when we deconstruct their false worlds, because that is all they have. If you've built your whole life around your job and your reputation, you naturally don't want to let go of them. You will fight not to die. Ultimately, however, the naming and dismantling of the false self is profoundly liberating—but we have yet to learn that.

In spirituality, there are basically two paths: the path of the fall and the path of the return. The path of the fall is directed and legitimated by the prophets, who teach us how to go into shadows creatively, how to let things fall apart. They teach us how to lose gracefully, how to let go without fear.

The role of the prophet is to direct and legitimate necessary deconstruction, the deconstruction of what I would call the false self. The prophet's path is of descent, and is never popular, nor easy. It is about letting go of illusion and toppling false gods. The prophets are always killed.

The other path is the path of the return. That's been the role of the priestly class. True priests talk of union, communion, love, transcendence, religion, connecting this world and the next world, and giving back a coherent world of meaning. Everybody usually likes the priests and they quickly become established and comfortable in almost all cultures.

We've had way too much priesthood and not nearly enough prophecy, in my humble opinion. The result often has been religion for religion's sake, all path of the return with no path of the fall. How can we return to a new world when we have never fallen away from the old one? Priests tell self-satisfied people about communion with God, yet their God and their need is still so small, or even false. How can we know the light if we've never named the shadows?

Twelve

A Reconstructionist Creed

Let us end on a hopeful note. Let us, as Saint Francis said, begin again. Allow the following creed to inspire our efforts to rebuild.

We believe in one God. "There is one Body, one Spirit, one and the same hope . . . one Lord, one faith, one baptism, one God who is Father of all, over all, through all, and within all" (Ephesians 4:4–6).

We believe that we are, first of all, a people, God's movement in history.

We believe that our individual lives and our personal growth are built on the faith and the bones of those who have gone ahead of us and lived for the sake of the generations to come after us.

We believe that we must build on the positive, on what we love. Creative life-energies come from belief and commitment. Critics must first be believers who have learned how to say an ultimate "yes."

We agree to bear the burden and the grace of our past. We agree to honor what is, which includes even the broken things of life: ourselves, church, state, and all institutions. The shadow side of each of these is a good and necessary teacher.

We are committed to building a world of meaning and hope. We recognize the clear need for prophetic deconstruction of all idolatries that make the worship of God impossible. True rebuilding must follow this temporary but necessary unbuilding.

We believe in a personal universe where the divine image shines through all created things. It is therefore an enchanted universe where we can always live in reverence and even adoration before the good, the true, and the beautiful.

Like Paul (in Colossians 1:15–20), we believe that Jesus is the clearest image of the unseen God. In him, all things cohere, all opposites are overcome. He is the head of the living body in whom all things are reconciled and overcome.

Epilogue

"You see the trouble we are in: Jerusalem is in ruins . . . Come, let us rebuild the walls of Jerusalem and suffer this indignity no longer." . . . "Let us start building!" With willing hands they set about the good work.

—Nehemiah 2:17–18

Brothers, let us begin again, for up to now we have done nothing.
—Saint Francis of Assisi

Endnotes

1. Walter Brueggemann, *Spirituality of the Psalms* (Minneapolis: Fortress, 2002), 9–11.

2. Daniel Breazeale, trans. and ed., *Fichte: Early Philosophical Writings* (Ithaca, NY: Cornell University Press, 1993), 63.

3. G. I. Gurdjieff, *Beelzebub's Tales to His Grandson* (New York: Penguin, 1950), 138.

4. Paul Ricœur, *The Symbolism of Evil* (Boston: Beacon, 1967), 351.

5. Stephen L. Carter, *The Culture of Disbelief: How American Law and Politics Trivialize Religious Devotion* (New York: Anchor, 1994).

6. Michael Lerner, *The Politics of Meaning: Restoring Hope and Possibility in an Age of Cynicism* (New York: Perseus, 1996).

7. Teresa of Ávila, *The Interior Castle*, trans. Mirabai Starr (New York: Riverhead, 2004).

8. Andrew Robinson, "Thus Spake Albert," *Aeon*, March 12, 2018, https://aeon.co/essays/why-do-we-love-to-quote-and-misquote-albert-einstein.

9. Elizabeth Barrett Browning, "Aurora Leigh," in D. H. S. Nicholson and A. H. E. Lee, *The Oxford Book of English Mystical Verse* (London: Oxford University Press, 1917), https://www.bartleby.com/236/86.html.

10. William Blake, "The Little Black Boy," https://www.poetry-foundation.org/ poems/43671/the-little-black-boy.

11. Andrew Greeley, "Oh, to Be a Victim," *The Tablet* (March 1, 1997): 283.

12. Ibid.

13. Ibid.

14. Ibid.

15. Francis Thompson, "The Hound of Heaven," Nicholson and Lee, *English Mystical Verse*, https://www.bartleby.com/236/239.html.

16. Ewert H. Cousins, *Bonaventure and the Coincidence of Opposites: The Theology of Bonaventure* (Chicago: Franciscan Herald Press, 1978).

17. Thomas Merton, *Thoughts in Solitude* (New York: Farrar, Straus and Giroux, 1958), 79.

18. Richard Tarnas, *The Passion of the Western Mind: Understanding the Ideas That Have Shaped Our World View* (New York: Ballantine, 1991).

19. Ralph Waldo Emerson, *The Essential Writings of Ralph Waldo Emerson* (New York: Random House, 2000), 262.

20. Bonaventure, *The Life of St. Francis of Assisi*, trans. E. Gurney Salter (New York: E. P. Dutton, 1904), II, 4.

21. The Rabbi of Ger, as quoted in Martin Buber, *The Way of Man: According to the Teaching of Hasidism* (New York: Citadel, 1994), 33.

22. Aleksandr Solzhenitsyn, "A World Split Apart," Commencement Address, Harvard University, June 8, 1978, https://www.americanrhetoric.com/speeches/alexander-solzhenitsynharvard.htm.

23. See the monumental works of spiritual intellectual Ken Wilber in this regard.

24. Abraham Lincoln, "First Inaugural Address as President of the United States," March 4, 1861, https://www.bartleby.com/124/pres31.html.

25. Miguel de Unamuno, *Tragic Sense of Life* (New York: Dover, 1954).

26. Romano Guardini, as quoted in Gerard Noel, *The Anatomy of the Catholic Church: Roman Catholicism in an Age of Revolution* (New York: Doubleday, 1980), 13.

27. See Richard Rohr, *What Do We Do with the Bible?* (Albuquerque: CAC Publishing, 2018).

28. See Michael Dwinell's especially fine book, *God-Birthing* (Liguori: Liguori, 1994).

29. David Ray Griffin, *Spirituality and Society: Postmodern Visions* (Albany: State University of New York Press, 1988), 16.

30. Bill McKibben, *The Age of Missing Information* (New York: Random House, 1992).

31. Mahatma Gandhi, https://www.goodreads.com/quotes/ 40054-there-are-people-in-the-world-so-hungry-that-god.

32. C. G. Jung, "Transformation Symbolism in the Mass," *Collected Works of C.G. Jung* (Princeton: Princeton University Press, 1969), II:201–296.

33. See Walbert Bühlmann, *The Coming of the Third Church: An Analysis of the Present and Future of the Church* (Maryknoll: Orbis, 1976).

34. Ambrose Bierce, *The Devil's Dictionary* (London: Arthur F. Bird, 1911), https://www.gutenberg.org/files/972/972-h/972-h.htm#link2H_4_0004.

35. Charles Williams, as quoted in Raymond Hockley, "In the City and Under the Mercy," *Sage* 79, no. 668 (March 1976): 97.

36. See especially the documents on the Church and the decree on non-Christian religions found here: http://www.vatican. va/archive/hist_councils/ ii_vatican_council/index.htm.

37. Thomas Jefferson, letter to William Smith, November 13, 1787, https:// www.loc.gov/exhibits/jefferson/105.html.

38. John Stuart Mill, *On Liberty* (London: John W. Parker and Son, 1859), 95, italics added.

39. For more on this topic, read my books *From Wild Man to Wise Man: Reflections on Male Spirituality* (Cincinnati: Saint

Anthony Messenger Press, 2005) and *Quest for the Grail* (New York: Crossroad, 1994).

40. Robert Inchausti, *The Ignorant Perfection of Ordinary People* (Albany: State University of New York Press, 1991).

41. Jean Houston, *A Mythic Life: Learning to Live Our Greater Story* (New York: HarperCollins, 1996), 98.

42. Saint Augustine, *Ten Homilies on the Epistle of John to the Parthians*, Tract VII, 8.

43. I address this in *From Wild Man to Wise Man* as I attempt to understand the Promise Keepers Movement and the "heroic" needs of the young male.

44. A line from the nursery rhyme "Humpty Dumpty," which traditionally refers to an egg.

45. Kenneth Clark, *Civilisation: A Personal View* (1969; London: BBC, 2005), DVD.

46. Daniel Goleman, *Emotional Intelligence: Why It Can Matter More Than IQ* (New York: Bantam, 1997).

47. See especially Gerald May, *Will and Spirit* (New York: Harper & Row, 1982).

48. Teresa of Ávila, *The Interior Castle*, Fourth Mansions, II:3.

49. Libreria Editrice Vaticana, *Code of Canon Law* (Washington: Canon Law Society of America, 1983), http://www.vatican.va/archive/ENG1104/_P3C.HTM.

50. Dennis Linn, Sheila Fabricant Linn, and Matthew Linn, *Good Goats: Healing Our Image of God* (Mahwah: Paulist, 1993).

51. T. S. Eliot, *Four Quartets* (New York: Houghton Mifflin Harcourt, 1943), 14.

52. Ibid, 15.

53. Ibid, 15–16.

54. T. S. Eliot, *The Waste Land* (San Diego: Harcourt Brace, 1922), 4.

55. Ernest Becker, *The Denial of Death* (New York: Free Press, 1973), 57.

56. Robert Browning, "Pippa's Song," *The Oxford Book of English Verse: 1250–1900*, ed. Arthur Quiller-Couch (Oxford: Clarendon, 1919), https://www. bartleby.com/101/718.html.

57. Arthur Lovejoy, *The Great Chain of Being* (Cambridge: Harvard University Press, 1936).

58. Bonaventure, *The Soul's Journey to God*, I, 9, emphasis added.

59. Meister Eckhart, *Consideravit Semitas,* Sermon on Proverbs 31:27. See *The Complete Mystical Works of Meister Eckhart*, trans. and ed. Maurice O'C. Walshe (New York: Crossroad, 2009), 275.

60. Bonaventure, *The Soul's Journey to God*, 1, 14.

61. Ibid., 5, 8.

62. Ewert H. Cousins, ed., *Bonaventure: The Soul's Journey into God* (Mahwah: Paulist, 1978), 32. The idea comes from Alan of Lille.

63. Bonaventure, *The Soul's Journey to God*, 1, 15.

64. Ken Wilber, *A Brief History of Everything* (Boston: Shambhala, 1996).

65. Ken Wilber, *Sex, Ecology, Spirituality: The Spirit of Evolution* (Boston: Shambhala, 1995).

66. Wilber, *A Brief History of Everything*, 293.

67. Friedrich von Hügel, *The Mystical Elements of Religion: As Studied in St. Catherine of Genoa and Her Friends* (New York: Crossroad, 1999), 69.

68. David Tracy, *The Analogical Imagination: Christian Theology and the Culture of Pluralism* (New York: Crossroad, 1985).

69. Hilaire Belloc, "The Catholic Sun," https://allpoetry.com/The-Catholic-Sun.

70. Ken Keyes, Jr., *Handbook to Higher Consciousness* (Berkeley: Love Line Books, 1993), chapter 3, emphasis added.

71. *The Autobiography of G. K. Chesterton*, ed. Randall Paine (San Francisco: Ignatius, 2006), 99.

72. Library of Congress Prints and Photographs Division, Washington, http://hdl.loc.gov/loc.pnp/ds.13124.

73. As quoted in Paul Johnson, *A History of Christianity* (New York: Touchstone, 1976), 275.

74. John Barth, "Night-Sea Journey," *Esquire*, June 1, 1966, https://classic.esquire.com/article/1966/6/1/night-sea-journey.

75. Doc Childre and Howard Martin, *The HeartMath Solution: The Institute of HeartMath's Revolutionary Program for Engaging the Power of the Heart Intelligence* (New York: HarperCollins, 1999).

76. Matthew Fox, *Meister Eckhart: A Mystic-Warrior for Our Times* (Novato: New World Library, 2014), 184.

DISCOVER MORE OF
RICHARD ROHR

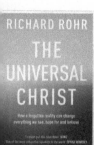
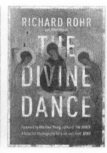

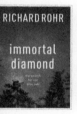

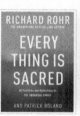
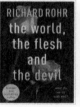
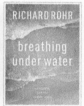

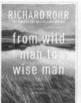

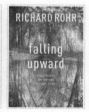